ESSENCE
OF
COVENANT

Copyright © 2017 George Benjamin

All rights reserved. No part of this publication may be produced, distributed, or transmitted in any form or by any means, including photocopying, recording, or other electronic or mechanical methods, without the prior written permission of the publisher, except in the case of brief quotations embodied in critical reviews and certain other noncommercial uses permitted by copyright law. For permission requests, write to the publisher, addressed "Attention: Permissions Coordinator" at the email address below:

Life and Success Media Ltd
e-mail: info@abookinsideyou.com
www.abookinsideyou.com

Unless otherwise stated, all scripture quotations are taken from the Holy Bible, New King James Version. Quotations marked NKJV are taken from the HOLY BIBLE, NEW KING JAMES VERSION. Copyright © 1973, 1978, 1984 by International Bible Society. Used by permission of Hodder and Stoughton Ltd, a member of the Hodder Headline Plc Group. All rights reserved. "NKJV" is a registered trademark of International Bible Society. UK trademark number 1448790.

Quotations marked KJV are from the Holy Bible, King James Version.

Cover Design: MIADesign.com

"I will give you a new heart and put a new spirit inside you: I will take the stony heart out of your flesh and give you a heart of flesh. I will put my (Holy) Spirit inside you and cause you to live by my laws, respect my rulings and obey them." Ezekiel 36:26-27 CJB.

I will make a covenant of peace with them, an everlasting covenant I will give to them, increase their numbers, and set my sanctuary among them forever. My home will be with them; I will be their God, and they will be my people. The nations will know that I am Adonai, who sets Israel apart as holy, when my sanctuary is with them forever." Ezekiel 37:26-28 CJB.

CONTENTS

FOREWORD - 7
PREFACE - 10
DEDICATION - 12
THE BEGINNING - 13
NEW SIDE OF GOD'S GLORY – The First Adam - - - - - - - - - - - - - 17
NAMES - 23
GOD'S MASTER PLAN - 26
THE PRINCIPLE OF COVENANT EXCHANGE - - - - - - - - - - - - - 42
EDEN THE CENTRE OF LIFE - 49
THE WORLD OUTSIDE - 53
THE COVENANT AT WORK - 57
AUTHORITY - God (The Living Water) has chosen us - - - - - - - - - 68
OBEDIENCE - 70
THE POSITION OF KINGS - 74
THE UNVEILING ROLE OF THE HOLY SPIRIT - - - - - - - - - - - - 76
THE DECLARATION - 80
SPIRITUAL CREATIONS - 84
OBSERVING THE TEMPLE
RULES FOR VERIFYING A HEALING - - - - - - - - - - - - - - - - - - 87
YESHUA AND THE FATHER ARE ONE - - - - - - - - - - - - - - - - - 90
THE AUTHORITY AND OBEDIENCE OF CHRIST - - - - - - - - - - - 92

THE MIND OF THE MESSIAH	97
THE REVEALED SONS OF GOD	101
SATAN THE ADVERSARY	107
JESUS OUR HOPE	110
SONS	111

FOREWORD

I have known George Benjamin for many years and have a deep respect for him as a brother in Christ. George has a very real and active faith which has been and continues to be demonstrated by the way he has responded to through very testing and adverse conditions.

Therefore a great deal of thought has gone into the content. One is also aware of the dependency George had on the Holy Spirit to bring revelation, to guide and to inspire him.

The book is very comprehensive in its treatment and understanding of God's original purpose, this being that we should be His sons and daughters. George promotes this point with strength and clarity and one senses this is very special to him.

It is a very challenging and thought provoking book. George promotes some very interesting thoughts which cause you to think through your own viewpoint and understanding of what he is trying to convey to the reader.

I believe a grasp of this teaching is one of the most liberating and healing truths that can come to the people of God.

As you read, study and contemplate the contents of this very interesting book, I am sure it will be a great blessing to you and move you on in your understanding of what it means to be a son or daughter of the living God.

Terry Diggins
Pastor
Plaistow Christian Fellowship

It is said of Caleb (Numbers 14:24)… because he had another spirit with him and hath followed me fully.

But I wholly followed the Lord my God (Joshua 14:8). Forty years old was I when Moses the servant of the Lord sent me from Kadesh-barnea, to spy out the land. (Joshua 14:7).

Verses 10-11: And now behold the Lord hath kept me alive as he said these forty and five years… As yet I am as strong this day as I was in the day that Moses sent me. As my strength was then, even so is my strength now for war, both to go out and to come in; at 85 as strong as at 40 and full of health and strength. I have known the author Rev. George Benjamin for a long time, and know him to be a man with another spirit. One who has fully followed the Lord.

I have been blessed by his ministry and deem it to be a privilege to write this foreword.

I trust these pages will cause you also to follow the Lord wholly and have another spirit to receive the fullness of the blessing of the Lord.

Rev. F. Collier
Glad Tidings Tabanacle

PREFACE

I would acknowledge my appreciation to all for their support and prayers which have enabled me to publish and print this manuscript.

The study of Essence of Covenant has benefited from many voices over the 6 years of preparation of this manuscript. Rev. Benjamin spent much time in prayer and fasting seeking the mind of God yet open to critical and constructive responses of those who have had a substantial impact on his own thinking about the significance of The Essence of Covenant.

I would like to thank all those whose comments and questions led to beneficial rethinking and reworking; for the time and effort they gave in reading various portions of the manuscript and supplying vital critique and support.

Firstly to our daughter Pastor Brenda Heron, who among others had been the first to receive the manuscript for her perusal, and though currently undergoing extreme pressure was able to provide vital comments and critique, my grandson Samuel Nugent who has been a tremendous support, and a pillar of strength, my son John Benjamin for his support offering computer skills and advice, daughter Minister Georgia Scotland for her assistance during the final stages of the manuscript, when portions had to be read and reread due to careful grammatical corrections before final approval, my nephew Dean Philogene a pillar of support when on the verge of discouragement, and to Sis Irma Vidal for her kind assistance in presentation of a summary of the book.

My most profound thanks to my son-in-law Pastor Dennis Scotland of WGMI for his support and consistent good advice having read the manuscript and provided encouragement when I needed it most.

DEDICATION

Thanks to the Holy Spirit who after 8 years has made it possible that another facet of His wisdom and revelation can be revealed through The Essence of Covenant. To God be all the Glory.

On behalf of my husband Rev. George Benjamin I dedicate this book to the Benjamin family and the body of Christ…….those with a passion for revelation and truth.

Rev. Benjamin has gone to be with the Lord but "his works follow after him."

"I have no legacy to leave except that Christ be instilled in the hearts of His people" …. Rev..George Benjamin.

Senior Pastor Elaine Benjamin
Co.Founder
WGMi

THE BEGINNING

Our great God and Creator desired to establish a permanent creation, which from its origin would reveal a new facet of His glory, not yet revealed to any of His created beings in their dispensation. Far beyond human comprehension, this revelation of His brilliance would unfold countless aspects of the mysterious wisdom of God, plus the depth and riches of His glorious love for the human race He was about to create. This feature of God's brilliance, to be revealed only at the birth of His new family, He called "Covenant;" a guarantee that His plans for the human race would be fulfilled.

God clearly confirmed His plan in the Garden of Eden, where at the beginning of creation, He introduced and set in motion, natural principles, and procedures for the man and all that he was about to create.

Man - His Form and Nature

And God said, "Let us make man in our own image, after our own likeness...so God created man in His own image, in the image of God created He him..." (Gen.1:26-27 KJV).

That man would be created tri-partite, body, soul, and spirit to reflect the Trinity of God is only one facet of His true intention, however, God is Spirit, and can only be revealed as such, therefore the true image He intended to reflect was the righteous holiness of His Son Jesus (Yeshua), which is total obedience and honour unto the Father.

Throughout the scriptures, and in particular, the book of Daniel (Dan.7:3-7) and Revelation (Rev.13:1-4) we see that all the created beings are described differently in terms of their respective order and roles. Though they were given different forms when sent by God to bring messages to man, yet they were all similar in appearance. This would suggest that none of these beings had been created similar to human beings. However, the Eternal God, the Triune One, chose no other form for the creation of His sons and daughters but the reflection of His own image and likeness.

One can only look at the overall structure and principle of the kingdom of God throughout all the dispensation of the angelic beings which have been founded on obedience. The fruit of this type of obedience is manifested in holiness unto the Lord. This is the same for the dispensation of man and throughout the kingdom of future created beings.

The downfall of Satan was disobedience and we read in the scripture that this was also the cause of Adam's fall.

The scripture commands that we should be Holy as our Father in heaven is Holy (1 Peter 1:16).

It is only after Jesus had given a total commitment to the obedience of his Father's will, that the title "Lord" was bestowed upon Him, and the Father said, "this is my beloved Son in whom I am well pleased" (Matt.3:17 KJV).

The apostle Paul admonishes us saying "let your attitude toward one another be governed by your being in union with the Messiah Yeshua" (Phil.2:5 CJB).

Divine Nature Attributes (DNA)

God also introduced and encoded, through a sovereign act a divine law, as the foundation and essence which would guarantee the fulfilment of His divine purpose and intention for the spiritual well-being of the man, and others for all eternity.

Man was given a human spirit which would enable him to carry the divine nature and attributes of God, His very DNA. This would allow humans to have eternal life and empower them to live in Holiness which, as discussed earlier, is the founding principle of the Kingdom of God. The word Yeshua in Hebrew means Salvation. Being encoded with the DNA of Jesus, would enable man through the Holy Spirit to recognise God, and operate in the same manner as the Father, the Son and The Holy Spirit, i.e. in His "image" and "likeness."

Yes! He stamped His indelible superscription into the spirit of man.

God intended that human beings possessed the same characteristics of personality, thinking patterns and attitude as His son Jesus. At the right time, He would activate those divine nature attributes (DNA), which lay dormant in the human spirit of man. This DNA would only be activated when God's Holy Spirit entered into the human spirit bringing life to it. This action is what we call "born again" i.e. when the spirit becomes filled with Life, God's own life which is divine, eternal, and uncreated. This process allows us to become God's sons and daughters who would live with Him forever.

This is our DNA, the foundation and essence of God. He chose us to become the recipients of His Life and become His children, born in His own image and likeness.

The Fall

After the creation of Adam and Eve in Eden, God introduced natural principles and procedures for their spiritual well being throughout eternity. They were given authority over all things and commanded to be obedient in one specific area "...and the Lord God commanded the man, saying, of every tree of the garden thou mayest freely eat: but of the tree of the knowledge of good and evil, thou shalt not eat of it for in the day that thou eatest thereof thou shalt surely die" (Gen. 2:16:17 KJV).

"And they heard the voice of the LORD God walking in the garden in the cool of the day: and Adam and his wife hid themselves from the presence of the LORD God amongst the trees of the garden."

And the LORD God called unto Adam, and said to him 'Where art thou?' (Gen.3:8-9 KJV).

Having read the above scriptures, we see the signs of disobedience are beginning to surface as Adam and Eve hide themselves from God. It had been their custom to meet with their Father to have fellowship with Him in the beautiful environment He had prepared for them.

"Therefore the LORD God sent him forth from the garden of Eden ...." so He drove out the man and He placed at the east of the garden of Eden cherubim, and a flaming sword which turned every way, to keep the way of the tree of life" (Gen.3:23-24 KJV).

Due to the disobedience of Adam and his wife, God through the birth, death and resurrection of His Son Jesus Christ, introduced a divine law of Grace based on the principle of Covenant Exchange. This would be the foundation and core guarantee of total provision for this new creation, His New Order of Spirit beings, to be called "Man."

In order to validate this law, one could say that in the great counsel room on high, after discussion with the Trinity, God presented His plans for mankind.

NEW SIDE OF GOD'S GLORY

– The First Adam

When we look at the plan of redemption, we can see the revelation of a new facet of God's glory i.e. the omnipotent God undergoing a process whereby He becomes Triune, Three. The Hebrew word is "Echad" which numerically means "one." (Deut.6:4). God becomes The Man Yeshua the Messiah, His Son, and yet being God, The Father. **This representation was not to convey division as they continued to be co-existent, co-eternal and co-equal** in **three representations of One God,** but it allowed God to show us **how to relate to Him** by revealing Himself through the Godhead and maintaining its consistency i.e. God is God, the origin of life, through the man Yeshua, His first-born Son, He would live in a human body and have a human nature, and yet remaining in the eternal dimension of being God our Father.

This representation allowed the Father to fulfil His desire to have sons and daughters. This new side of God's glory was unprecedented because for the first time God, through His Son Yeshua, would live in a human body and possess a human nature. Remember that He is God and not man and does not think or operate as we do. He would maintain the consistency of the Godhead i.e. God is God – the origin of life; He is Spirit; and He is the Father of all Spirits.

In order to fulfil the desire mentioned above, we see the Spirit of God becoming Man in the person of His Son.

"God was in Christ reconciling the world unto Himself"
(2 Corin.5:19 KJV).

God is preparing to create Man, a new order of Spirit, different from all other created beings: man will be triune, and have a body, soul, and spirit; they will be God's sons and daughters, created in His own image and likeness.

Isaac typified Yeshua, who was the true Son of Abram, born in the house of his father. However, Jesus was conceived by the Holy Ghost in the womb of a virgin called Mary. The angel Gabriel who was sent to declare this covenant mystery to her, declared that "He shall be called the Son of God" (Luke 1:30-35 KJV).

He became the "First Born Son of God" (Heb.1:4-5 KJV; Psalms 8).

For God so loved the world that He gave His only begotten Son..... (John 3:16 KJV).

The word "only" was placed here by the Holy Spirit to emphasize the fact that the "Man Yeshua the Messiah" was begotten for the sole purpose of fulfilling the Father's eternal desire to have sons and daughters born of Himself. "Beloved now are we the sons of God" (1 John 3:2 KJV).

Jesus first presented in 'Types' and 'Shadows'
"Things which are a mere shadow of what is to come; but the substance belongs to Christ" (Colossians 2:17 The Ryrie Study Bible).

The Old Testament holds types and shadows of God's intended plan for a full relationship with us as His sons and daughters.

The scriptures reveal God meeting and holding discussions with His servants which would later reveal His plan for mankind.

God told Abram that his dynasty would be great and would come from his first son, Isaac. When Abram spoke to God concerning his childless situation, he mentioned Eliezer, who although born in his home, was not his child, and not being his own child, Eliezer stood to inherit everything! God answered "this man will not be your heir. No your heir will be a child from your own body" (Gen.15:2-5 CJB).

Later as promised, Isaac was born, who became a shadow of Yeshua, God's own Son who was born of The Father. He later declared in the book of John "This is my Son, whom I love; I am well pleased with him" (Matt.3:17 CJB).

The Angels are **types of sons** not by birth but by creation. They were created to serve and worship Him. When referring to angels, God "makes his angels winds (spirit) and his ministering servants flames of fire" (Heb.1:7 CJB). They are like Abraham's loyal servant Eliezer serving God faithfully in his house but not as sons. They are not rightful heirs to His kingdom as we are. Although they may be of a high rank, and called "sons of God", they cannot claim to be born of God. However, a son born of God is entitled to walk in His great house with kingly dignity and bring joy and satisfaction to His heart. In Job 1:6, we read that there was a time when the sons of God came to present themselves before the Lord and Satan came also.

As we look at created beings we see that they are called "sons" by right of their creation but not by birth. Hebrews chapter 15 supports this statement saying "for to which of the Angels did God ever say You are my Son: today I have become your Father." God has never said of any angel "I will be His Father and he will be my Son" (Hebrews 1:5 CJB). The angels are indeed unique beings, created by God to worship and serve in His kingdom. They are unable however, to reproduce themselves because of Eternal God's design and plan for them. However, His plan for His true Son Yeshua, following His death and resurrection, possessed the unique ability to replicate Himself by having sons and daughters born of Him.

Man – a type of God's First Fruit
From all His creation, the Almighty God has taken a tithe, a first fruit for Himself. Exodus 13:2. Man was chosen to be set aside as a tithe unto Him.

Of all the mighty galaxies of space, God chose the planet earth as the place set aside for His new order of spirit called man. There in the eastern section of Eden, God placed man in His garden prepared with His own hands. This He tithed unto Himself. One may conclude that, at the end of creation, man had been chosen to become a type of "tithe" unto God and to give Him glory. The bible tells us that God took six days to create the heavens and the earth and on the seventh day God rested, He set aside and "tithed" this day as His own (Genesis 2:3 KJV).

"Of his own will begat he us with the word of truth, that we should be a kind of "first-fruits" of his creatures" (James 1:18 KJV).

One may ask how can this be?

The eternal God is Omnipotent and Omnipresent. He is Alpha and Omega and abides in "the now", the ever present.

The question may arise, how do you know that God chose man to glorify Him before future creations. I may ask, will there ever be another man Yeshua the Messiah who came from the Godhead, or will there ever be another "Begotten Son"? My answer is "I do not think so."

Jesus when praying to His Father on behalf of His disciples said "I have given to them the glory and honour which you have given me...I in them and You in me" (John 17:22-23 KJV).

Adam and Christ

As we review the Old Testament, we discover further "types and shadows." Adam called the "first Adam" was earthy meaning that he was a "shadow" of Yeshua; a prototype of God's intended Plan who would be created from the earth. God breathed life into him i.e. gave him a human spirit and he became alive. When the time came for the birth of Christ and all spiritual events were in alignment, Father God sent His first born Son Christ, called the "second Adam." Jesus came with the Life, which would allow Him to have sons and daughters born and **not created** and fulfilled His Father's Plan.

Noah and Christ

As a second example of "types" and "shadows", we later see this Covenant principle in operation in Noah's life where deliverance comes in the "type" or form of the Ark! This was a covering which saved an entire family from death. We read in Genesis 6:17-18; "behold, I even I am bringing the flood of water upon the earth; to destroy all flesh in which is the breath of life from under heaven; everything that is on the earth shall perish. But I will establish My Covenant with you; and you shall enter the ark – you and your sons and your wife, and your sons' wives with you" The Ryrie Study Bible. On leaving the Ark and stepping out on dry ground, Noah offers an animal as a sacrifice to God, and upon accepting the sacrifice God promises never to flood the earth again and seals His Covenant with the sign of a rainbow. The rainbow reminded God of His promise never to destroy the whole earth with water again.

Isaac and Christ

In the Old Covenant, Isaac is presented as another "type and shadow." During a conversation with God (Genesis 15:2-4) He reassures Abram that the promised child Isaac would be heir and not his servant Eliezer.

"And behold the word of the Lord came to him, saying; This man shall not be your heir, but he who shall come from your own body shall be your heir."

The angel Gabriel when he appeared to Mary declared that Yeshua would be called "the Son of God" – God's first born son. We read in Hebrews 1:1-2 "in the past God spoke to our ancestors through prophets at many times and in various ways, but in these last days He has spoken to us by His Son, whom He appointed heir of all things, and through whom also He made the universe." New International Version.

Now we can really understand John's exclamation of both our present and future existence when he claimed: "see what love the Father has lavished on us in letting us be called God's children. For that is what we are. The reason the world does not know us is that it has not known Him." Dear friends, we are God's children now; and it has not yet been made clear what we will become. We do know that when he appears, we will be like Him; because we will see Him as he really is (1 John 3:1 CJB).

NAMES

The importance of His Name signifying Position and Title

In Jewish custom as far back as the early biblical forefathers, we see that names were significant, they had meaning and much more than a title. On many occasions, Abraham called God by a new name, which signified the way in which he had met God. Names were not the only means of identifying God, but also the different ways in which He presented His heart (essence), character and position to His people.

The Apostle Paul tells us that Christ inherited a superior position and name over the angels. This was given by His Father. I use the word "inherit" to present the understanding that this honour could only be given to a son or daughter (Hebrews 1:4-5). What is this "name" or "title"? Is it Jesus? No, because the name "Yeshua or Jesus" reveals His ministry and work as our Saviour. Is it then "Lord"? The scripture tells us "and that every tongue will confess that Jesus Christ is Lord, to the glory of God the Father" (Philippians 2:11 KJV). Again I would say no, as Jeshua was given the title of "Lord" because of His obedience to the Father by going to the cross and releasing us from sin. He is to be called "the Son of God, The Son of The Highest" by the rightful inheritance of BIRTH.

The angel Gabriel said to Mary that the child was to be called "Jesus... the Son of the Highest" (Luke 1:31-32. KJV). This name would be more excellent and superior to all other names given to every created being. The Apostle Paul also tells us that "God also hath highly exalted him, and given him a name which is above every name. That at the name of Jesus every knee should bow, of things in earth, and things under the earth;...." (Phillipians 2:9-10.KJV).

Hebrews 1:4 makes it clear that the glorious Name (title) which He has inherited is different from, and more excellent than theirs, For to which of the angels did God ever say: You are My Son, today I have begotten you, established You in an official Sonship relation, with kingly dignity? And again, I will be to Him a Father, and He will be to Me a Son? Hebrews 1:5 Amplified Bible. We read further in verse 6 "And again, when He brings the firstborn Son again into the habitable world, He says, Let all the angels of God worship Him." Notice the word **again** suggests all created beings worshipped Him from the time of His conception to His becoming a son in glory. This would be throughout eternity.

His Name – ELOHIM

God has placed us in a position that is higher than any other angelic being. In Psalms 8, we read that human beings were made a little lower than God. The King James version originally translated God as: "angel" however the original Hebrew translates the word as: "Elohim" meaning God. The Almighty, The Creator and Judge of the Universe. The adjectives "little lower" reminds us that our Father is always greater than us, His children.

In Psalms 110, we read "The Lord (God) says to my Lord (the Messiah), Sit at My right hand, until I make Your adversaries Your footstool." Amp. Bible.

Our Name – Son

Psalms 8 continues to describe our inheritance and title as sons by saying that this title comes with authority over all God's creation on earth. It explains that God "put all under His feet." In John 17, in His prayer to the Father, Jesus says that He has given us the Glory and the Honour which God has given to Him: The Holy Spirit is now in us and Christ is united with the Father. God's fullness lives in us. His Magnificence!

His name – YAHWEH (Jehovah)

God does not live in the past or future, but in the continuous present. When Moses asked about His name, God revealed His name saying; I AM WHO I AM AND WHAT I AM – I WILL BE WHAT I WILL BE (Exodus 3:13-14 The Amplified Bible).

The Hebrew word YAHWEH means the Ever Present God. In other words God said to Moses tell them that the Ever Present has sent you.

God's eternal plans exist in Him. When we think of future **events, they are taking place in God's present.** The bible tells us that God speaks about things which have not taken place in our lives as if they have already taken place in our present. The eternal God is Omnipresent and Omnipotent. He is Alpha and Omega and abides in "the now", the ever present

GOD'S MASTER PLAN

When God planned to create man, it is important to understand that this conversation mentioned above in Gen 1:26-27, did not take place in Eden but in heaven's throne room, where there was total agreement among themselves, The Father, The Son, and The Holy Spirit (1 John 5:7 KJV).

It was necessary to hold this discussion before the creation of the world, because of the effect on the wellbeing of man, his continuity, and above all his salvation.

A master plan through a process of "Covenant Exchange" would enable man to love God freely.

The Father's family would take on the same form as Himself; they would be just like Him, reflect His nature though created from the "dust of the earth", yet they would be a unique creation of spiritual sons and daughters.

"I will give you a new heart and put a new spirit inside you; I will take the stony heart out of your flesh and give you a heart of flesh, I will put my Spirit inside you and cause you to live by my laws, respect my rulings and obey them" (Ezekiel 36:26-27 CJB).

"I will make a covenant of peace with them, an everlasting covenant I will give to them, increase their numbers, and set my sanctuary among them forever. My home will be with them, I will be their God, and they will be my people. The nations will know that I am Adonai, who sits with Israel apart as holy, when my sanctuary is with them, forever" (Ezekiel 37:26-28 CJB).

It appeared that the Holy Spirit allowed Ezekiel to hear a conversation in the "Great Throne Room" long before we were created. This was a staggering plan in its design, not revealed to the present created beings.

The bible tells us that the angels are crying "Holy, Holy, Holy", as they stand in amazement and diligently observe this awesome plan of God (Rev.4:8-11 KJV).

. Before the creation of man, there was a Man in heaven who represented all of Adam's sons but would later become God's sons. It was essential that God pass through this process. He is Sovereign and chose this way to permanently establish Yeshua's Lordship and righteousness over every Order of created beings, including us, the mankind. This process would show that Yeshua's name is superior to all other names as we read in Ephesians 1:19-21 "and what is the surpassing greatness of His power toward us who believe (KJV). These are in accordance with the working of the strength of His might, which He brought about in Christ, when He raised Him from the dead and seated Him at His right hand in the heavenly places. Positioned far above all rule, and authority, and power, and dominion, and every name that is named, not only in this age but also in the one to come."

What an amazing plan God put into place for us, His new creation, His New Order of Spirit called "Man", who would be totally different from all other creations He had made.

In order to complete His plan our Eternal Father had to go through a procedure which would **maintain the consistency and authority of the Godhead and show that He is God, the Creator of everything seen and unseen. He is the Beginning and End of all creation in Eternity. God is Spirit and all his creations are spirits and He remains God, The Father of all spirits.** Now He is preparing to create human beings; a new order of spirit and totally different from all his previously created beings. This man would be matchless and triune having a body, soul and spirit. Above all this man, and all those to follow, would become the Father of His sons and daughters made just like He is.

GRACE

To fulfil such a plan, God, in His divine wisdom, conceived, and birthed "Grace." This would reveal a new facet of His glory to be experienced only by mankind. This "Grace" would be one of three major components of the "birth, death, and resurrection of Jesus Christ" which God was about to use to enable man to evolve into His image and likeness. One often refers to "Grace" as God's unmerited favour however, it was designed to represent The Almighty God living in us through the Holy Spirit. Jesus promised to send the Holy Spirit after He left earth. His work allows us to take part of the life of Yeshua to portray His character. Through Grace we experience His divine love in various aspects of our lives.

Therefore we can say that Grace is God's mighty indwelling presence in His children.

Grace is a subject, an entity, God dwelling in us by the Spirit of His Son, the Holy Spirit, which allows us to partake of the abundant riches of His very life in us.

The subject Grace produces character, personality, and integrity, its object produces power, purpose and the various ways whereby we become affected by it.

As a result, we become lost for words and express our emotions by saying "we don't deserve God's unmerited favour."

The Apostle Paul on three occasions pleaded with God to remove the 'thorn' from his 'body' however, the Lord replied by saying to Paul, "my Grace is sufficient for thee....upon me" (2 Corin. 12:9 KJV). The Lord reassured Paul by saying that His powerful life called the Holy Spirit who dwells in him is able to comfort and sufficient to make him strong on the occasions when he felt weak. **Grace is God's mighty life, the Holy Spirit living in us.**

It is a free and perfect gift which we receive without struggle or hard work. The angelic beings unable to understand it, stand amazed as they behold the wondrous glory of the eternal God dwelling in man.

Experiences of Grace – Soweto, South Africa

I remember clearly two very special encounters I had with the Holy Spirit during our ministry in South Africa. My wife Elaine and I had completed an intensive two weeks of teaching in the town of Phalaborwa and its surrounding areas, and were looking forward to a well earned rest. We had spent a few days in Johannesburg with a dear friend who was the pastor of a church in Soweto. He took us on a tour of the area and to the place where the first black boy was shot by the police during the South African race riots. This resulted in large numbers of young people being killed; eventually we visited an area where hundreds had been buried in mass graves.

Our first encounter with grace at work was during our visit to a mother of the church who was respected both in the community and the church. Having heard so much about this township, we anticipated visiting with great excitement. From a distance the town appeared to spread for miles, however, nothing could have prepared me for the level of abject poverty and squalor which greeted us as we drove through Soweto. My heart broke, and I was filled with compassion as we passed multiple rows of shacks made of either cardboard boxes or for the more fortunate ones, tin sheets. I was appalled to observe a group of children playing beside a large steel tank where open sewage flowed freely. My thoughts asked God how people could possibly live in such conditions.

The car stopped and we were led through what appeared to be an unending maze of shacks made up of either mud, cardboard, or flattened tin sheets. Finally we arrived at the lady's home where she was seated outside on a small wooden stool. As we came nearer, she stood with great excitement, bowed and invited us in. While she sat on the stool, what followed was a brief conversation between herself and the pastor in the regional language.

I glanced towards the tin shack where she lived and noticed that her home was conspicuously clean. The walls were lined with newspaper; to the right lay a bed sectioned by a crisp white sheet to mark her privacy. The dirt floor was spotless and to the left lay about five cardboard boxes stacked vertically, used as storage for the kitchen wares. Beside the boxes stood a small cooking primer stove. It was difficult not to think about the luxuries I take for granted at home, compared to the bare necessities which reflected this woman's standard of living.

This gracious woman then began to share with my wife and I, her relationship with God, her love for Him coupled with her experience of the deep satisfaction and joy in knowing Him. Her very countenance shone with the glory of God, reminding me of Moses after he had an encounter with God on Mount Sinai. Here she was living in a tin shack in Soweto situated in the most notorious township in South Africa, yet she possessed something I craved for, a living experience of God's Life. On that day it was indeed true that a 'life giving river' was flowing through her which impacted us with life changing consequences.

I could see that it was God's grace through the Holy Spirit which had filled her life, and found this so overwhelming, that I called out to God to give me the same substance which allowed "someone" to reveal the expression of His life. She was able to 'tap' into unlimited resources of spiritual wealth which excelled far beyond her everyday circumstances.

We had experienced a deeper encounter with our Everlasting Father in the most deprived area in South Africa.

Wealth

Following this encounter, the Holy Spirit taught me the secret of being satisfied with a peaceful mind. Wealth can be defined as the overwhelming richness of God's Spirit, the presence of the Messiah living in us! This is Grace. As we left her home that day, over and over my thoughts cried out to God to give me what she had!

Paul's passion was to know God, and have a deeper understanding of the power which brought Him back to life. He had a strong desire to understand this wealth and defined Grace as a "treasure in earthen vessels, so that the surpassing greatness of the power will be of God and not from ourselves" (2 Corin. 4:6-9 CJB). God heard Paul's prayer and gave him this same power through the difficult yet successful experiences in his life. Paul refers to this treasure as the Holy Spirit who carries the light of Yeshua the Messiah who Himself radiates God. He is the 'light' who makes us aware of our Father.

For it is God who once said "Let the light shine out of darkness," (Gen.1:2-3 KGV) made His Light to shine in our hearts through Yeshua the Messiah. It is this treasure in 'clay jars' that we find overwhelming power to support us in troubled times, housing in us, the embodiment of God's Grace.

"For God, who commanded the light to shine out of darkness, hath shined in our hearts, to *give* the light of the knowledge of the glory of God in the face of Jesus Christ. But we have this treasure in earthen vessels, that the excellency of the power may be of God, and not of us" (2 Corithians 4:6-7 CJB).

Paul describes our like experience as "troubled on every side, yet not distressed, we are perplexed, but not in despair; persecuted, but not forsaken; cast down, but not destroyed; always bearing about in the body the dying of the Lord Jesus, that the life also of Jesus might be made manifest in our body" (2 Corin. 4:8-10 KJV).

Not only was Paul aware of the indwelling Holy Spirit, but he relied on this mighty power in every circumstance of his life. Paul therefore strongly encourages us to come boldly to God's Throne of Grace.

The Throne of Grace
"For we have not a High Priest which cannot be touched with the feelings of our infirmities, but was in all points tempted like as we are, yet without sin."

"Let us therefore come boldly to the throne of grace, that we may obtain mercy, and find grace to help in time of need" (Heb.4:15-16 KJV).

Historically a throne is a stately symbolic place where laws were passed by kings and queens, and declarations made. It was also the place where final judgement, and appeals were made to overturn decisions, some serious as life or death. The Sovereign had the final authority over any decision. God set His Son Yeshua the King ruling from the throne called 'Grace.' Unlike earthly kings, Yeshua identified with our everyday life. He touched sadness, temptations, and human emotions beyond a level we would never experience. Paul reminded us that Yeshua is our "High Priest" an Advocate who though tempted to sin as we are yet did not give in to such desires.

Located at the Grace Throne is the mercy seat where Yeshua our Great High Priest has guaranteed to meet us, and offer forgiveness for our sins whether big or small. When the lyricist asked the question "what can wash away my sins?" I believe the Holy Spirit emphatically answered him saying "nothing but the blood of Jesus!" At the Throne of Grace, God's loving arms will always support His children, and carry us on eagles' wings. He knows exactly what we need and has established His throne guaranteed by His precious blood (Hebrews 4:16). The Law of His Throne is 'Grace' which is the substance of His divine nature and attributes (Refer to GRACE).

Dear reader I would encourage you to go boldly to the Throne of Grace for mercy and help in times of your need, make it your home. No one has the final word on your life, and future, and you can appeal against every adverse judgement made against you. **Go boldly to God for His final decision.**

Examples of Grace

When Zechariah met God's Angel who revealed the timing of this great event "then he answered and said unto me, saying: Not by might nor by power, but by my Spirit, says the Lord of Hosts."

"Who art thou, O great mountain? Before Zerubbabel thou shall become a plain: and he shall bring forth the headstone therefore with shouting, crying, Grace, Grace unto it!" (Zechariah 4:7 KJV).

"And I will pour upon the house of David and upon the inhabitants of Jerusalem, the spirit of grace and of supplications..." (Zechariah 12:10. KJV).

John the disciple and prophet, on seeing Christ shouted "this is the man I was talking about when I said the one coming after me has come to rank ahead of me because He existed before me....We have all received from His fullness, yes grace upon grace...For the Torah was given through Moshe; grace and truth came through Yeshua the Messiah" (John 1:15-17 CJB).

Grace is layered on grace, and there is even more grace! God has prepared all the grace we will need to take us through every testing situation in our lives. All we need to do is bodily approach God's Throne of Grace with trust. There we will find all the help we need to carry us through testing times! The bible reminds us that Moses brought God's law to the people (Deut. 31:12) then Jesus fulfilled the prophecies spoken of Him and brought Grace.

The bible tells us that people went to God's Throne of Grace to receive mercy. In Exodus 25: 17-22 we see the detailed specification given by God concerning the building of the mercy seat.

God instructed Moses to place the mercy seat on top of the Ark. He assured Moses that He would meet him there for a discussion and instructions; that He would be located between the two Cherubim above the Mercy seat.

Hannah and Grace

Hannah was confident of God's promise, and guarantee when she applied to the Throne of Grace. In a distressed state she found help when she pleaded to the Judge of the Universe, the only one who had power to intervene, end her pain, and enable her to have a child. God blessed her with a boy who she named 'Samuel.' He was no ordinary man but one chosen to be God's prophet, the first of his kind (1 Sam. 1: 1-28 KJV).

King David and Grace

On several occasions, David went to the Throne of Grace to appeal to God to save him from his powerful enemies (See Psalms 35:1 KJB). He was able to praise God for his victories through divine intervention, Psalms 43:1-5 KJB. **Your victory is assured at God's Throne of Grace and Mercy.**

King Hezekiah and Grace

There was King Hezekiah, who was warned by God through the Prophet Isaiah that he had a terminal illness. The bible tells us that Hezekiah "turned his face to the wall" (2 Kings 20:2 KJV). He went to the Throne of Grace, and tearfully appealed to God to save his life, reminding Him that he had lived his life in truth with a perfect heart. God answered immediately through Isaiah saying that He had heard Hezekiah's prayer, seen his tears, and extended his life by 15 years.

And the Lord said through the prophet Isaiah "tell Hezekiah I have heard thy prayer, I have seen thy tears: behold, I will heal thee" (2 Kings 20:5 KJV). Hezekiah was healed. No one was able to reverse Hezekiah's fate but God. He had appealed to the Throne of Grace where the faithful God had promised to meet His children. He reminded God that he had lived his life in truth and with a perfect heart. Amazing Grace was extended to him. God's mercy, compassion, and clemency flowed from His heart; Hezekiah's life was saved. **God will answer us when we pray. His Spirit will never leave us.**

Does God change His Mind?

You may ask the question: did not God say "For I am the Lord, I change not;....." (Malachi 3:6.KJV). Yes He did, however, God was referring to those unchangeable essential qualities and attributes which allow us to identify with His character and traits as the only true and living God. This did not refer to the way in which He deals with human beings, but His response to those who are obedient and love Him. In such cases, God promised to be with them and would turn away only when they chose to disobey. We look at King Saul as an example. God blessed Him when he chose to obey, however, problems followed when he disobeyed. The bible tells us that God 'repented' having chosen Saul as king because he disobeyed His commandments.

We read also of the evil heart of man, when God repented that He had made man on earth; "and God saw that the wickedness of man was great in the earth and that every imagination of the thoughts of his heart was evil continually" (Gen.6:5 KJV).

"And it repented the Lord that He had made man on the earth, and it grieved Him at His heart."

And the Lord said I will destroy man whom I have created from the face of the earth. Both man and beast, and the creeping thing, and the fowls of the air, for it repenteth me that I have made them" (Gen 6: 6-7. KJV)

The KJV version uses the word "repent" which is the Hebrew word "Nacham" meaning 'to groan', 'to be sorry', 'to breathe strongly (sigh), 'to repent.' The Greek word "Metanoia" means 'a change of heart based on a change of mind.'

This word 'repent' is an anthropomorphism, a word metaphorically used to allow God to express human emotions such as anger, which allows us to relate to this side of His character. Therefore the word 'nacham/repent' means that God, on these occasions, chose to change His course of action **based on man's change of heart.** God judges on the basis of His word; He judges us when we disobey, grace and mercy when we obey. We continually change our minds; God does not. 'I am the Lord I change not.'... (Malachi 3:6 KJV).

Job and the Throne of Grace

The bible tells us about Job who was afflicted in his body, however, he made his bed at the Throne of Grace, there we see the marvellous way in which God took him through events which challenged the very core of his belief. However, Job finally came to the pinnacle of his sufferings when he triumphantly declared: "O that my words were written in a book! O that they were printed in a book!"

That they were graven with an iron pen and laid in the rock forever! For I know that my Redeemer lives, and that He shall stand at the latter day upon the earth. And though after my skin worms destroy my body, yet in my flesh shall I see God: whom I shall see for myself and my eyes shall behold and not another; though my reins be consumed within me" (Job 19:25-27 KJV).

Jonah and the Throne of Grace
This list could go on and on! Please make your own study. Look at Jonah, and God's amazing grace to him at His Throne of Grace in the belly of a whale. Grace is the mighty indwelling presence of the Triune God and this gift is sufficient for you. God said that He would give us a new heart and a new Spirit. He would remove our hard heart and give us a heart which responds to His call on our lives (Ezekiel 36: 2-27; 37:26-27).

How close is God to you? He is anywhere you are and ready to hear your call.

Grace in Kenya - An Invitation
My second experience took place in Kenya, East Africa. I had been speaking in a town called Eldoret for a period of six weeks, when I was invited by a pastor from overseas to speak on a Sunday morning, to a large congregation at a local church. The meeting was being held in one of the large function halls in the finest hotel in Eldoret. That morning, my interpreter Hurun arrived early at the venue and introduced me to the pastor who I had not met previously. She outlined her vision for the ministry followed by the order of service for the day. After a brief conversation, she then left to meet other people. This allowed time to sit

in the hall and pray. During that time, I estimated around two hundred people had gathered. As I looked around it became quite evident that I was among affluent people and though I truly believe that our heavenly Father desires us to prosper in every area of life, yet He expects us to have a humble heart.

I was called to speak and began by introducing myself followed by the scripture reference from Hebrews chapter 4 :12, and commenced speaking. After twenty minutes, I sensed that the word was not getting through, and my spirit was in warfare. It appeared that I had faced a brick wall, sensing intimidation, and opposition to the word. In my spirit, I called to God asking Him what was happening, and why I sensed such opposition. I needed an immediate response from Him, however, He remained silent. I could sense the word as 'bouncing off brick walls' of opposition returning to me. I must admit that in all my years of ministry in many countries around the world, this was the first time that I intentionally, and immediately cut a sermon so short. I did not call people for prayer but abruptly concluded the message, returned the microphone to the pastor and sank into my seat next to Hurun. As I sat there, I continued to call out to God asking Him to explain what had happened. I received no answer.

After the service, and brief words with the pastor, Harun and I left the hall. We headed outside the hotel, and reluctantly towards to a place where the host pastor had prepared meals for us.

During lunch, Harun asked whether I would accept an invitation to speak at the church of one of the pastors who had attended an earlier outdoor service which had taken place that week. He stressed that he would understand if I declined to accept as the church was located in a squatter camp. As he waited for my answer, I considered his request. I was still perplexed and unsettled by my earlier 'ordeal' still waiting for the Lord to answer me on the two previous occasions. However, as I sat locked in thought I could feel the Holy Spirit gently persuading me to go. I accepted the invitation.

We took a taxi as far as the journey would allow then took a short walk to the area. I quickly realized the reasons why Harun had offered me the choice to attend. Slowly emerging in front of me was a vast sea of huts made from every conceivable type of material which possessed a mere hint of potential to build a home. The rainy season increased the challenge to the tough environment which transformed the entire area to a slaghead of mud. To add to the hostility of the environment, a pungent smell wrapped itself around my head which appeared to deprive my lungs of air. I tried to manage small intakes of breath as I hurriedly followed Harun through the camp. My stifled breaths revived memories of my youthful days in my native country, when my friends and I would go diving in the blue Caribbean waters, each waiting to see how long we would stay under water then surface gasping for air, however this was under quite different circumstances.

As I walked, there were a number of happy children who played in gutters filled with mud and water. Thoughts of degradation then arose which starkly contrasted the backdrop a few miles away where others lived surrounded in luxuries. I continued walking gasping for air and wondered whether their bodies were immune to the innumerable diseases present in what I could only describe as an inhumane environment. In my heart I asked God whether there was any hope for these people, and a future for their children?

I enjoy photography, and always take a camera to capture and document my travels. I use pictures as visual prayer reminders. As I reached for my camera, suddenly, I heard the Holy Spirit say in an abrupt manner, 'No! Do not take any pictures here, you must respect the dignity of the people.' I immediately put my camera into my bag and asked His forgiveness.

We finally left the area, climbed a hill where we began to breathe normally and view the entire squatter camp. As we approached the top of the hill, I could hear the voices of singing and in the distance we viewed a small round mud hut. On arrival we were greeted with a warm welcome by the pastor, and a few men. The hut was filled to capacity. I estimated around forty people were present sitting on floor mats, and low wooden stools. A small table served as a pulpit, and light radiating from the sun filled the small area.

Stooping through a small doorway, I followed Harun and the host pastor. I felt God's overwhelming presence, and as I looked, I saw Jesus sitting on the floor at the right hand side of the table. His awesome presence filled that little mud hut on the top of the hill. The people were filled with joy, and as they worshipped and praised, the wonderful love of Yeshua brought healing and deliverance to all who needed it. There was no need to speak, as we stood and worshipped in the presence of the Lord, He spoke to me "I dwell among the humble, I dwell among the humble." There the Lord revealed to me a deeper understanding of **The Essence of Covenant** through the Holy Spirit,

'Thus saith the High and Lofty One that inhabits eternity, whose name is Holy, I dwell in the high and holy place, with him also that is of a contrite and humble spirit, to revive the spirit of the humble and to revive the heart of the contrite ones' (Isaiah 57:15 KJV).

I was amazed at the reality that the omnipotent and majestic God could so humble Himself to be with people in the squalor of a ghetto camp. I was also amused at the time and location the Lord chose to answer my prayer. In His infinite wisdom, He plans our lives, and through His Holy Spirit, allows us to encounter life experiences which forge the divine nature and characteristic of His Son Yeshua the Messiah.

I worshipped Him through my tears as I considered His Grace which I was able to understand later. With the 'benefit of hindsight' I can now appreciate the reasons why, in a single day, He took me from a place of wealth to one of extreme poverty. Without criticism of each experience, I realised the reason was to develop His divine nature in me!

After the service was over we stood at the top of the hill looking over the camp; there I heard the Holy Spirit say "now you can take a picture of the camp." God promised that He would live in us, a 'building' not made with hands but one which had been 'birthed' and prepared by His own Son. We are the temple where God lives. He said 'I will dwell in them and they will be my people' (Rev.21:3 KJV).

King Solomon speaking to the Lord during the dedication of the temple cries out in sheer amazement at God's desire to dwell in man "will God indeed dwell with men on earth? behold, heaven and the heaven of heavens cannot contain thee" (2 Chron.6:18) yet God was preparing to come and dwell in a temple not made with hands, but one birthed and prepared by His own Son for Him: that is the temple called "man" the dwelling place of God.

THE PRINCIPLE OF COVENANT EXCHANGE

In order to accomplish Grace, God introduced Covenant, which was founded on the principle of exchange of our weaknesses for His strength. The word 'exchange' means "to give up, to part with, or to transfer one thing." The word transfer means to change, or go from one thing, person to another. When God created mankind, in His divine knowledge, He foresaw Adam's fall, and conceived a 'Covenant' plan to present His Grace.

God conceived a plan in order to reveal a covenant exchange. Yeshua would give up His life for our weaknesses and frailties. His Son from the Godhead, born in the womb of a young virgin girl called Mary, would be given such titles as Wonderful, Counsellor, The Mighty God, The Everlasting Father, (Isaiah 9:6) Emanuel, God with us in human form.

He would take our sins upon Himself and make us free from guilt and condemnation to death. As a result of our acknowledgement of Him as our Saviour, and acceptance of the shedding of His own blood for us, He would forgive our sins and cover us with His righteousness. We could then enjoy our relationship with God, our Father. His Holy Spirit would then fill our lives, enabling us to become His sons and daughters. We would carry His name and the character and qualities of His Son. Isaiah 53 paints a description of God's Son, and explains that as part of the covenant, we could transfer our grief and sorrows onto His shoulders in exchange for peace and healing.

Our established rights as God's Sons
It was necessary that this covenant be made through God's righteous Son Jesus, not by any other created being such as Adam and his wife. Eve was

taken from Adam's side while he was in a 'deep sleep.' This was a shadow of God's covenant and master plan (Gen.2:18-23).   Years later, Yeshua would sleep 'the sleep of death' for three days (John 2:19-21). In this plan, we who represent Eve (also known as His Bride) are taken from the side of Christ, revealing our new birth as His 'Sons' and 'Daughters.' When the soldiers who stood by the cross pierced His side, the bible tells us that 'blood' and 'water' (John 19:34) gushed out representing His humanity, divinity, and the birth of His children into a new and eternal life. It was after Adam had seen Eve, he could to say 'this is now bone of my bone and flesh of my flesh' (Gen.2:23). In other words "she is like me."

We would complement God when we came from within Himself just as Eve came from Adam and Isaac from Abraham. It would be the 'modus operandi' (method of operation) He would choose to give birth to His sons and daughters.

What a blessed mystery, that the omnipotent God, the Ancient of Days, the Supreme Creator of all things, the Omnipresent One, who resides in all times and dispensations, chose you and I to be like Him.

David was amazed by the ways in which he had witnessed this work and cried saying "Oh God this knowledge is too great for me, it is beyond my ability to understand it" (Psalms 139:6).

The question could be asked 'what knowledge did Yeshua have to carry our sins?' We must remember that He knew the plan of the Father before the foundation of the world. This plan was discussed in the great Throne Room. Secondly, when the plan was 'conceived,' our Father gave birth to the 'Grace and Covenant Exchange' explained earlier. Lastly, Yeshua by giving His life, the benefits, and blessings of the covenant would be accomplished and set in motion. According to His word, God has the legal right to live in us through the person of His Holy Spirit. There are answers to all forms of questions, or accusations by any created beings past, present, or future concerning our new title of 'Sons of God.' We will carry His name through the ages to come. As an example, think of a boy who despite of all his developmental changes, continue to carry his father's name through generations. God used this new side of His Glory to create His Master Plan. This plan had never been revealed to any of His creations (1 Peter 1:12), but kept hidden in His heart also known 'as the volume of the book' (Heb.10:7; Psalm.40:7).

By this knowledge, Jesus went to a cruel cross, dressed as the Covenant Lamb to deliver us through the principle of Covenant Exchange. He exchanged our sins for His righteousness, and brought into effect, the operation of "Covenant" as the Father had planned a long time ago. Isaiah prophesied "therefore, I will allot Him a portion with the great, and He will divide the booty with the strong, because he poured out himself to death, and was numbered with the transgressors" (Isaiah 53:11 Ryrie Study Bible).

David reminds us saying "Many, Oh Lord my God, are thy wonderful works which thou have done, and thy thoughts which are toward us..." (Psalm 40:5 KJV). We are inheritors of all that belongs to Him with whom we will rule, and reign with the King of kings.

The Process of Time and God's Plan
God speaks of future events as if they have already been accomplished or are presently taking place. The bible tells us that "...and calleth those things which be not as though they were" (Romans 4:17.KJV). We call the Father's heart 'the secret place' as seen in Psalms 91 "...that dwells in the secret place of the most High shall abide." Eternity and time comes from the heart of God and He is in total control. He uses His perfect timing to bring into effect His divine will, and bring glory to His name. He remains the author of time through the countless ages of eternity.

If we take this into consideration, one could ask this question: As Yeshua had been chosen to be our Saviour, what choice did Adam and

Eve have when we consider that God gave them the choice to "choose life," knowing that they would choose "death?"

However, God had already prepared a plan whereby He would make complete provision for their deathly choice. Revelation 13:8 KJV tells us that Jesus was 'slain' before His death took place on earth. He was submissive to the will of His Father when He said that He had come to fulfil the plans concerning Him which had been foretold in the scrolls. "......but a body hast thou prepared me: ...in burnt offerings and sacrifices for sin thou hast had no pleasure. Then said I, Lo I come (in the volume of the book it is written of me) I have come to do thy will, O God" (Hebrews 10:5-7 KJV). The scrolls had foretold what would happen. What was the "will" which Jesus came to fulfil? This was His Father's plan that He would be the Covenant Lamb who was chosen to make the 'exchange.' He would take our sins and iniquities in exchange for the indwelling of His Holy Spirit, (Zoe); the divine eternal life of the Father. We now become His sons and daughters who have been born of His spirit.

This is the Essence of Covenant, the result of God's Covenant

Hebrews 5:9 states 'and being made perfect, He became the author of eternal salvation unto all them that obey Him.' The significant word in this sentence is 'eternal.' Yeshua the Messiah became the author of our 'eternal salvation.' This speaks not only of our salvation from sin and death, but from the eternal, unimaginable consequences of never being able to share the excellent honour of being an heir with His Firstborn Son, Jesus. (Refer to Hebrews Chapter 1 for further details of Yeshua's title, position and inheritance).

The term 'first born Son' refers to Jesus, and we understand that He is the Father's first Son. It also portrays the birth of many other sons. We learn in Romans 8:29 that God knew us before we were born and chose us to be His sons and daughters. In this plan, it was God's desire that we would take on and grow in the characteristics of our big brother Christ Jesus. We have an inheritance which gives us the right to possess all that belongs to Him. When we meditate on this eternal indescribable glory it is not difficult to join with John's joyful statement "beloved, we are (even here and now) God's children, it is not yet disclosed (made clear) what we shall be (hereafter), but we know that when He comes and is manifested, we shall (as God's children) resemble and be like Him, for we shall see Him as He really is" (1 John 3: 1-2 Amp. Bible). John appeared to be saying that this type of love was incredible and staggers our imagination.

In John chapter 17, while praying to His Father, Jesus the 'Only Son' who became the 'first begotten' of many sons says: "All things that are mine are yours, and all things that are yours belong to me; and I am glorified in them. (They have done me honour, in them my glory is achieved).

I have given them the glory and honour you have given me, that they may be one (even) as we are one" (John 17:10:22 Amp. Version).

The term 'all things', does not refer simply to material 'things' such as the works of His hands, but to the excellent glory of the omnipotent God.

This is all that God is
The Devil, our enemy who tempted and deceived Eve to disobey, is now confronted with this very issue of honour and inheritance. He now faces eternal contempt, and separation from God, without hope of ever becoming a Son; he has lost the honour which God intended for him. We cannot understand the ramifications of such punishment, but can try to imagine the indescribable horror of it all. This eternal judgement is the cause of Satan desperately seeking to destroy as many lives as possible.

God's Sons and Daughters on the Earth – Gifts

Through various writers inspired by the Holy Spirit, the bible gives us an understanding of our identity, yet making it clear that the Father has not fully disclosed what we will be like after this life (in the eternities to come) (1 John 3:12. Amp. Bible). However, one event is certain, we will be changed to reflect Christ Jesus.

When we accepted God into our lives, His Holy Spirit filled us, and activated His DNA, His divine nature and attributes which had been sealed in us in Eden. This action resulted in a gradual change which enables us to reflect His own image. By the plan of redemption through our Lord and Saviour Jesus Christ, God who is the master of diversity, has given us a unique expression of Himself which enables us to express in a particular way, His exceptional facet and magnificent glory. **We reflect God's face** (Romans: 8 v 29).

The apostle Paul refers to the gifts of the Holy Spirit, 1 Corinthians 12:28-31 KJV; facets of His glory, i.e. the gifts of healings, the word of wisdom, the workings of miracles, in addition to the different areas in which we are called to work in God's kingdom i.e. evangelists, prophets, pastors, teachers. These gifts of the Spirit we received from His DNA at the time of creation. An example is the "gift of tongues;" it is the language of the new born spirit man, with which our spirits speak to our heavenly Father, making us able to communicate with Him through the power of the Holy Spirit. These speech sounds are unrecognisable to others, however when we ask God, He will give us the ability to understand what we are saying so that we may 'interpret' to the church whatever message He reveals. The apostle Paul teaches that we should pray for the interpretation. This gift is for comfort, consolation, guidance and exhortation to enable us to communicate God's messages in other languages (1 Corinthians 14:2-3 KJV).

The supernatural gifts of healings, the working of miracles, and the gift of faith, express God's power. As mentioned above, we have received these gifts in Eden when Adam was created as part of God's DNA. They lay dormant as a result of the fall of man, however, when our spirits came alive they were stirred by the Holy Spirit now living in us. They are facets of God's glory which He gives to help those in need. Jesus became an heir to all the Father possessed, and because we have become joint heirs with Him, now possess all that the Father has given to His Son. In Christ's last prayer, as seen in John 17, He prayed 'I have given to them the glory as you have given to me.' What was this glory? The glory of being the Son of God! Hebrews Chapter 1 v 4 speaks of His glorious title as the Son of God, and we, His Sons walk in obedience and call Him Dear Father!

"For you did not receive a Spirit of slavery to bring you back again into fear, on the contrary, you received the Spirit who makes us sons and by whose power we cry out, Abba, that is Dear Father.

And if we are children, then we are also heirs, heirs of God and joint heirs with Messiah – provided we are suffering with Him in order also to be glorified with Him" (Romans 8:14-17 CJB).

EDEN
THE CENTRE OF LIFE

One may consider that Eden contained the genetic code for all God's creation where every species had been produced "after its own kind," e.g. trees produced trees, and animals produced animals. This pattern of reproduction is identical to that of man. However, as man was created by the Lord in His own image and likeness, his level of creativity, and intelligence far exceeds that of his environment; he portrays God's nature and character, and is able to function to his maximum potential by using his five senses. Man carries God's Genetic Code.

The bible tells us that God "breathed into his body the breath of life and Adam became a living soul" (Gen. 2:7.KJV). After his creation, we learn that God blessed Adam and Eve (Gen.1:27-28) who He had created in "His own image"; a pattern of reproduction similar to that of the animals, every species producing "after his kind" (Gen.21:24 KJV). Adam became a spiritual being, and was able to use his intellectual skills to the highest level in areas of discernment and revelation and could exercise authority over everything in Eden with one exception (Gen 2:16-17).

The animals, which were created before Adam, possessed a body but not a spirit. They are classed as a lower form of life. However, when God created man he was given a body, soul and spirit. We need a body to communicate and relate to the world through our five senses, taste, touch, vision, smell, and of hearing. The soul is often referred to as the centre of our emotions and character while the human spirit as 'the breath of life.' This is the spirit which God gave to Adam to allow his body and soul to come alive. I refer to it as God's 'seed' which elevated Adam above all other creation and gave him authority and responsibility over every animal. It is important to understand that the Holy Spirit is the 'water' which allows the human spirit to produce righteousness. We can view the human spirit as the 'womb' with the embryo symbolising 'righteousness' surrounded by its protective water. We now understand that the human spirit which God had prepared, was designed as the place where He would live in relationship with us and satisfy His passion to be a Father with a family born in His own image, and carrying His name.

The Covenant Exchange

It is difficult to fully comprehend, and ever be able to fully understand the mind of God. He controls the past, present, and future. He sees our misjudgement of events, yet forgives, and forgets our sins through the shed blood of Jesus our Deliverer. With this Truth in mind, God who is Omniscient, knew the choice of Adam, before His creation in Eden. The ability to choose is the most precious quality God has given to man; Adam was given the choice either to obey or disobey. Sadly he chose to disobey, which resulted, as discussed in the previous chapter, in the introduction of God's **Covenant Exchange and His Grace**, the unmerited favour of God.

Grace, God dwelling in Person in redeemed man through His Holy Spirit.

We see the first symbols of promise in Eden, the location for the establishing of the Covenant of Promise. The Eternal God who is all wise knew that Adam would choose to disobey His commands before he was created. In His excellent wisdom, He made a Covenant between Himself and the man. This superb plan would guarantee a relationship which would be stronger than death. It would be founded on the life of His Son Yeshua. This plan took immediate effect after the fall of Adam. God was neither astonished by the fall of Adam, nor can it be said that He had been at a loss as to His next plan. There had never been a 'Plan B.'

From the beginning of creation, it had always been the plan of God that man should have a mutual relationship with Him. Adam and Eve forfeited this right because of disobedience. This resulted in unimaginable distress as they realised that that they had failed their Creator. Looking on their nakedness (symbol of shame and failure), they searched for materials to cover themselves, and finally settled with.... "fig leaves" (Gen.3:7 KJV). Let us consider that the man and woman are now pitifully standing before the Triune God not knowing that His Covenant is unfolding before them.

The Death of the Animal
The book of revelation explains that Jesus, also called the Lamb of God, was killed before the world was created. The first symbol of the death of Christ, was the killing of an innocent animal whose skin was used to cover Adam and Eve (Gen 3:21 KJV). This provided protection, warmth and security as we recall that blood was shed. It is important to note that the symbol of the animal's skin was a type and shadow of the death of Christ about to take place years later (Rev. 5:6). This event had already taken place before the world was created. However, it had not been manifested on earth as this Covenant, made by the Triune God, had not been revealed. It was designed to be a process which would enable man to become His Sons and Daughters.

As discussed earlier, God made them clothes from an animal's skin, a symbol of the shedding of blood and death of an innocent animal in order to cover not only their shame and guilt, but also that of others. This process of clothing Adam and Eve, covered in the skin of an animal, would be a portrait of the emergence of His pre-planned Blood Covenant. This would be a shadow of the forgiveness of sins, complete deliverance, resulting in "abundant life" (Ezekiel 16:6;16:8 KJV). Through this covenant, just as the marriage covenant, we would take not only His name, but also His indwelling Spirit. In exchange we become submissive to His will and that of the Father. This Covenant Exchange, we would receive by faith, because of God's Grace dwelling in us. The promises of God never changes.

THE WORLD OUTSIDE

Life outside Eden would be a harsh existence. Adam and Eve are now exposed to all dangers and attacks of the enemy. The skin of the animal would provide **first a level of covering and second, the defence.** However, the Almighty God in this great master plan had already made provision for them, that by looking on the covering of the animal, the blood that was shed, and the animal's skin used to cover their nakedness, He would remember His promise. They would receive power to live under the most extreme, and severe conditions, and be protected at all times from all types of dangerous threats to their lives.

The Role of the Holy Spirit
God is the possessor of Eternal Life. It had been the plan of God that we should be created in His image and likeness. As mentioned before, eternal life is not simply a state of mind or time factor, it is a Person, God, the Holy Spirit, divine and eternal dwelling in man through "Grace." When conversing with the Samaritan woman at the well, Jesus revealed to her the Life of the Father saying, "God is Spirit" (CJB) and NOT "God is a Spirit."

The Prophets spoke of the pouring out of God's Holy Spirit into humanity. The Greek word for spirit is 'Pneuma' meaning 'breath', 'a spirit' or 'life'. The Holy Spirit is God's own life – the Essence of who He is. He is Divine and Eternal, not created. He exists, and has neither beginning nor ending. He is the Alpha and Omega of all things.

The role of the Holy Spirit is to give us the life of our Father enabling us to become His sons and daughters, born of Himself i.e. His Holy Spirit.

In the book of Ezekiel 36:26-27 CJB, we read that God would eventually place His Spirit in us and later, as expressed in Joel 3:1 CJB, His Life would be poured out on everyone. Years before, the Prophets of the

Old Testament foretold and pondered on this great event. It had not been revealed to them, the timing and circumstance of this great prophecy. 1 Peter 1:12 tells us that even the angels were curious. CJB. Although the prophets would not experience the fulfilment of such prophecies in their lifetime, yet they died with this belief that God is a "God who keeps promises" (1 Peter 1: 10-12 CJB).

However, at the time of the Festival of Pentecost, 50 days after the Passover, The Holy Spirit (Ruach Hakodesh) was 'poured' into His disciples as they waited in the 'upper room.' The Spirit then flowed through their lives which changed our world.

The account of Matthew and Luke both describe the unfolding of this long awaited event. Following the word of God as delivered by the angel Gabriel, the Holy Spirit fills the young virgin Mary who becomes pregnant as foretold by the Prophets. The Angel Gabriel informs her that the Holy child when born would be called the Son of God (Luke 1:31-35).

The prophet Isaiah in chapter 61, when prophesying about this great event mentioned words which Jesus would later declare from the Torah Scrolls in the synagogue. **"The Spirit of the Lord is upon me, because the Lord hath anointed me to preach the Gospel of good news to the meek; He has sent me to bind up the broken hearted, proclaim liberty to the captives and the giving of sight to the blind and to open the prison doors to them that are bound..."**

We find further detail as we look into the book of John when baptizing at Jordan, he saw Messiah Yeshua coming and exclaimed "Look! There is the Lamb of God, who takes away the sin of the world!" John 1:29 Amp. Bible. John declares later that 'Jesus is the Son of God' (John 1:35-36 Amp. Bible). The Holy Spirit would later prepare and strengthen Jesus for His death. The New Covenant sealed in His blood would bring into operation the eternal plan of the Father.

An example of the work of "The Spirit" is seen when He strengthens Jesus while He battles with strong emotions working against His desire to do the will of the Father. "Father if you are willing, take this cup away from me; still, let not my will but yours be done" (Luke 22: 42 CJB).

The prime objective of the Holy Spirit is not to prepare us for heaven. This could easily be achieved at the time of conversion when we felt the 'most holiest.' We were so "in love" with God and totally prepared for heaven! However, this may come as a surprise - we were left to LIVE our lives and fulfil our mission. Jesus asked His Father do not take us out of this sinful world, but to keep us in such an environment empowered by His Spirit (John 17:11).

The primary work is to create the characteristics of Christ in us in order to become joint heirs with Him. "How do we become joint heirs with Him?"

Through the effective inner working of the Holy Spirit, His word changes our way of thinking as we become transformed by the renewing of our minds, "this is the Lord's doing and it is marvellous in His (our) eyes" (Matthew 21:42 KJV).

Years ago, I heard a story of a man who showed his friend around his fruit garden which contained a section with various types of trees. Upon leaving, the man's attention was drawn to a particular tree which produced different types of citrus fruits on its branches. He was amazed and asked his friend about it. His friend answered saying several types of citrus fruits had been grafted into the tree which had enabled it to produce different types of fruit.

Enquiring further, he asked 'what was the original tree' as it now produced various types of fruits, he could see lemons, tangerines, grapefruits, oranges and limes. He replied "it's an orange tree." Still curious about the tree he asked, "when will it grow orange trees?" His friend replied, "when the tree grows its own branches."

Throughout the years, I have thought about this story and its spiritual aspect. I have often made it the focus of my prayers asking God to help me to be a true representative of the fruit of His 'Tree of Life' and not a 'grafted imitation.' We learn that the Holy Spirit is working in us to create true branches of the vine and develop righteous characteristics. The Holy Spirit chooses to compare us to "trees of righteousness" planted by the Lord that we may produce much fruit that He may be glorified. Isaiah 61:3.

THE COVENANT AT WORK

After the death of Christ, Peter tells us that Jesus preached to those who had disobeyed God during the time of Noah (1 Peter 3:18-20). They died as a result, however, Christ preached His victory over hell, bearing witness of the Father's Righteousness and fulfilling the Promise to raise His Son from the dead. David, by revelation of the Holy Spirit, in his prophetic writings foretold the death and resurrection of Christ (Psa. 16: 8-10. Amp. Bible).

Peter refers to this Psalm, declaring that Jesus had fulfilled the Master Plan of His Father. He explains His death was not by chance or coincidence, that by dying He would give birth to a family of sons and daughters. The death of God's Son followed by the outpouring of His Holy Spirit on His children would bring the Covenant into operation (Acts 2:33 Amp. Bible).

We see a further description of the work of the Covenant. Peter reveals that if angels were unable to solve this mystery of the Holy Spirit dwelling in human beings, the gift of grace and salvation, therefore it was not possible that the apostles would comprehend it (1 Peter 1:10-12. KJV).

Jesus encouraged His disciples when He explained that all things would be made clear to them after they had received the Holy Spirit. In Acts 2:33, Peter begins to explain this mystery with ease and clarity, declaring the absolute faithfulness of the everlasting Father in three different ways:

First: Jesus was exalted to this glorious position at the right side of His Father (as seen in Ephesians 1:20-22 and Hebrews 7:22), the result of His faithfulness to the Everlasting Covenant made before the creation of the world.

Second: The Eternal Father had kept the promise made to His Son that He would not allow His body to lie permanently in a grave but would raise Him back to life, fulfilling the Covenant of Exchange (Psalm 16:10).

Third: Peter explained that the outpouring of the Holy Spirit, the proof of the Covenant promise, was the introduction of the "third phase" of His plan (Acts 10:44). God's master plan is now complete, the birth of His sons and daughters, the outpouring of His life in and through us to others. This is a witness that He is satisfied.

A thief was nailed to a cross next to Jesus. He was the first one to receive this covenant promise by becoming a son. He asked for forgiveness, Jesus responds by forgiving his sins and giving him a new life. This would enable him to escape the horror and reality of eternal death. After the brutal and shameful death on the cross The Messiah promises that he would live forever. Below is the dialogue found in Luke 23:39-43.CJB.

Then he said, "Yeshua remember me when you come as King." v.42

Yeshua said to him, "Yes! I promise that you will be with me today in Gan-Eden" (Luke 23:43 CJB).

While in the middle of physical agony and the fear of death, the thief is forgiven and becomes a Son of the Most High God. Although his body hangs dying on the cruel Roman execution stake, yet he receives the promise and his spirit lives on forever. **However, we must not forget that his body will later be restored and live again when Messiah returns! (1 Thessalonians 4:14-18).** Death robs us of our loved ones, friends and families, some in adverse circumstances, however, God has promised that this death is not final; that he will live forever! This is a comforting thought to know that it is certainly not over!

We see the second example of the covenant at work. Jesus is among His disciples whom He calls "brothers" and not friends or followers. He refers to them as brothers, changes their status and unites them to the Father. However, before His death, He called them "followers" and "friends." They are now given the unearned title of 'sons' which has no reference to gender (John 15:13-15 CJB).

After His resurrection we learn of a dialogue between Mary and Jesus. When Jesus revealed Himself, overcome with joy she attempted to embrace Him, however, she was restrained (John 20: 11-18 CJB). Here we see the Covenant of Sonship in operation. Yeshua said to her, "do not touch me, because I have not yet gone back to the Father, but go to my brothers, and tell them that I am going back to my Father, to My God and your God."

By this we understand that they had the same relationship with the Father just as Himself the "only begotten Son" who had become the "first begotten Son" from among many brethren.

The work of Covenant was the foundation for the cross, the consequence was death, which resulted in the burial and subsequent resurrection of Yeshua our Messiah.

Grace (at work)

In John 1, and Genesis 1, we learn that the Word was existent in the beginning. It was with God, and is God. Jesus, who is called "The Word" was with God from the beginning. Everything came through Him, and nothing was made without Him. The Word became a human being, and dwelt with us. And we saw His Shi'kinah, (His glory, His honour, His majesty), the Shi'kinah of the only Son of the Father, full of grace and truth.

John 1:16-17 CJB reads "We have all received from His fullness, yes! Grace upon grace."

"For the Torah (the law) was given through Moses; grace and truth came through Yeshua the Messiah."

Grace and truth came through Yeshua the Messiah, that is, the indwelling presence of God became a reality because of Jesus.

Yeshua the Word is also known as The Light who carries Life and this Light shines in a dark, unbelieving world, (refer to v. 4-5) but it is not put out by its darkness. John goes on to explain that although Jesus was human, yet just as we do, He experienced the daily challenges of life. He had been rejected by His own people, however, through acceptance in His actions and words, we earned the right to become children of God. This He did by pouring out His Holy Spirit into us. In Chapter 1 v 16-17, John explains that 'we have all received of His fullness, yes, Grace upon Grace!'

After the children of Israel had left Egypt, according to the law which had been handed to Moses, God promised that they would receive blessings when they had obeyed His instructions, but curses if they chose to disobey (Deuteronomy 28 KJV). However, after the laws under the Old Covenant had been replaced by the New, and prophecies concerning Messiah had been fulfilled (John 5:39 KJV) the sacrificial system came to an end; we then received Grace and forgiveness through the High Priest, Jesus and His Holy Spirit who gives us the power to obey His instructions and live!

Grace is the Holy Spirit working in man

His Holy Spirit is now being poured out on all who believe. After His resurrection from the dead, Jesus told His disciples to wait a few more days until He had returned to heaven when the next phase of the plan of God would come into effect (Luke 24:29 KJV). In this phase, God planned to send The Comforter and Counsellor of His Holy Spirit His (Ruach HaKodesh) (Acts 2:1-4 KJV). We must remember that Grace and Truth came through Jesus. This was the very Presence of God, His Life, His Holy Spirit becoming reality in our lives (Ezekiel 36:26-27 & 37:26-27).

Jesus, The Perfect Sacrifice

We see in Genesis the journey of Abraham, who in obedience to the request of God was willing to sacrifice His only son Isaac (Gen.22:4-5 KJV, Hebrews 11:17 KJV). This was a challenging assignment, however, Abraham believed that God was able to bring him back to life. In effect,

Isaac was as good as dead! However, because Abraham fully trusted in God, one could say that Isaac was brought back from death. As Abraham is about to plunge the knife into his son, God appears and reveals a ram as a substitute sacrifice for Isaac (Gen.22:8 KJV).

However, there had been no sacrifice for the brutal and shameful way in which Christ died. Such death applied to slaves and soldiers who had been disgraced. There had been no rescue from the compulsory whipping and maiming; from the nails hacked into His feet and hands; the thorns gorged into His head. No miraculous escape from the sword which was stabbed into His side; no powerful angel appeared to prevent it, they watched unable to intervene. The sword pierced His body, through His flesh ripping open His heart, and caused blood and water to gush out. Read Isaiah 53; a Messianic prophecy now fulfilled, speaking of the death of Christ The Messiah, reveals this as the sacrificial offering of blood for our sins which would enable us to be free from the curse of sin and become the sons of God. In Ephesians 1: 3-6, and Hebrews 11:17-19, we are reminded that it was the plan of God, before the world was created, we were chosen to become His sons which would enable us to live daily before Him as a sacrifice! When the prophet Isaiah in chapter 53 makes mention to the "great and strong" v.12, he is referring to us, chosen of God before the world was created, to become joint inheritors with Jesus Christ.

The Spirit, The Soul and The Body

If we look closely at the scriptures, we understand that man is made up of three parts, body, soul, and spirit (Genesis 2:7.KJV). After death, our bodies, the physical part, goes back to the earth. Our souls, will return to God, if we obeyed Him while we're alive and "born again." This privilege we receive by the "Holy Spirit." "But God will redeem me from the power of Sheol (the place of the dead); for He will receive me." Psalms 49:15. Amp. Bible.

"Then shall the dust (the physical body wherein the spirit of man, the human spirit and the soul dwell) return to the earth as it was: and the spirit shall return to God who gave it" (Ecclesiastes 12:7. Amp. Bible).

However, those who disobeyed Him will remain in a place of torment awaiting judgment for their evil actions. The human spirit also known as God's 'breath of life', goes back to God, its owner.

God speaking through Ezekiel in chapter 18:4 declares "Behold all souls are mine; as the soul of the father, so also the soul of the son is mine; the soul that sins, it shall die" Amp. Bible.

This spirit, or 'breath of life' cannot be destroyed or contaminated by the actions of a person in his/her life on earth; it is the breath which came from God, it belongs to God and cannot sin.

Back to Adam
Adam was created with a body, soul, and spirit to reflect God, his Father. His soul was the first to become alive i.e. his personality, however, this was not the divine characteristics and attributes of God **found in the human spirit.** It is important to remember that Adam's body came first (see 1 Corinthians 15:45-47 KJV) while his human spirit lay dormant, but would later be made alive by God to reflect his true nature and splendour at the appointed time (Romans 8:2 KJV). The event would take place when God would send His Son, the second Adam, described as the "quickening Life Giving Spirit" (see verse 45).

The Role of Jesus the 'Life Giver'
Throughout the book of John, Jesus is seen as the "life giver." John declares that all things came into existence by Him and through His involvement. He declares that Jesus is "the Life and Light of Men;" the light which cannot be extinguished. See John 1: 1-5.KJV.

The bible reveals many names of Jesus, which allow us to discover who He is and the various aspects of His character.   John also records that Jesus is the "I am" (John 8:12 KJV); "The Bread of Life" (John 6:48 KJV); "The Light of the World" (John 8:12 KJV); "The Resurrection and The Life" (John 11:25 KJV); "The Way, The Truth and The Life" (John 14:6 KJV); "The True Vine" (John 15:1 KJV); and much more!

After Jesus was resurrected, He returned to His disciples, breathed upon them, and said "receive the Holy Ghost (Spirit)" (John 20:22). For the first time, the New Testament records the Holy Spirit dwelling in humanity. This allowed their human spirits to be 'born again' and made them followers of Yeshua. They were transformed from natural to spiritual men, true sons of God. Their dormant spirit, the result of the sin of Adam, is now able to express aspects of God's perfect attributes, the divine qualities which He had received in Eden.

This historical day, which had been spoken of by the prophets hundreds of years ago has now arrived; "the birth of the true sons of God!"

As Aaron's rod when it budded (Numbers 17:1-10), the righteous seed began to develop, effecting change in their character. They now have the Spirit of God living in them through which Life will go on throughout eternity! (Read 1 Corinthians 15:46, 49). It is only the Spirit of God who is able to give life and sustain His nature in us (John 6:63).

We really are unable to grasp the immense pleasure, and satisfaction of such event, the Holy Spirit breathing on man (John 20:22), had brought to the Father; the level of praise, worship and glory given to Him by His angels as they watched with amazement. The Almighty God who is Spirit would live in us! We can now truly understand the statement used by Paul when he described the Holy Spirit as a 'treasure' inside human beings. This has always been God's heart for us (2 Corin.4:7 KJV).

When teaching His disciples, Jesus said, "Just as the Father has sent me so I am sending you. If you forgive the sins of anyone, they are forgiven;

if you retain sins they are retained" (John 20:21, 23 Amp. Bible). What authority did Jesus possess? **He was sent with power over all creation and as The Saviour with authority to forgive sins.** When we read the story of the physically impaired man in Mark 2:1-5, we learn that **Jesus forgave sins.** The religious Jews who became incensed by this statement started to question His actions amongst themselves. They conclude by calling Jesus a 'blasphemer' for it is only God who can forgive sins. However, they failed to realise that Yeshua, the Son of God, was not an ordinary man, but one who had authority to forgive sins. Jesus, fully aware of their thoughts, asked whether it is easier to forgive the paralysed or heal him. With authority He puts His Spirit in His followers, giving them the power to forgive sins as fully fledged sons.

God gives us authority that we may be witnesses of His nature. Such is demonstrated through the Spirit who in turn directs our lives, and develops His perfect qualities. This work will impact our environment, homes, and places where we work.

Paul describes such qualities of God as the "fruit of the Spirit."

Love

The love of God is unconditional, and has been lavished on us through the ultimate sacrifice of His Son Yeshua. It is above all, the greatest (1 Corinthians.13).

Joy

The joy of the Lord, the Spirit, which is always present giving strength in all circumstances. In the Old Testament during the building of the temple, the prophet Nehemiah encouraged the people by exclaiming that the Joy of the Lord would be their strength (Nehemiah 8:10). The book of Proverbs tells us that "a merry heart is as good as medicine, but a broken spirit dries the bones" (Proverbs 17:22 KJV).

Peace

The God kind of peace which surpasses human understanding. It is like marrow which fills our spiritual bones, and keeps our spirits, and mind sound. It acts as a defence mechanism. Before He left His disciples, Jesus blessed them saying, "Peace I leave with you, my Peace, I leave with you, not as the world gives, do I give unto to you" (John 14: v 27). We can describe the peace of God as His Spirit which fills your soul and body, and enables your thoughts to be protected when you face the challenges of life.

Longsuffering

The quality of longsuffering which partners with 'joy' is an important attribute of being cheerful. It comes from the Greek word 'Makrothurmeo' which means long spirited, longsuffering, and to have long patience. The other Greek word "Hupomone," means cheerful, or hopeful endurance, constancy, and patient continuance. The fruit of longsuffering will enable you to endure the trials and challenges you face e.g. life's hardships or persecution without being worried, crushed, fearful or discouraged. This is because of His Spirit which strengthens you.

As mentioned above, longsuffering also means having an attitude of cheerfulness. When experiencing trials, the Holy Spirit will use this gift (cheerfulness) as the agent, which prevents us from being broken and discouraged.

As we allow God to lead us, we will be qualified as His mature sons and daughters (Romans 8: 9, 13, 14). Life in the Spirit will not be a "floating on air" experience, but a feature of our every day life where His DNA (divine nature attributes) is at work. Moses understood this principle and prayed that God would teach him His ways (Exodus 33:13).

Goodness

The nature of God which allows Him to provide for all creation. He makes the rain fall and the sun shine on both the just and the unjust, bad and good. His goodness extends to all and is experienced by all. We as His sons and daughters are able to extend the same to all, non-judgemental, and without partiality.

The prophet Isaiah declared "a bruised reed He will not break and a smoking flax He will not quench, He will bring forth judgement into truth" (Isaiah 42: 3 KJV).

Meekness (Humbleness)

Meekness will promote interaction with others from diverse backgrounds whether rich or poor, educated or uneducated, able bodied or physically impaired, the poor and the rich. Jesus commanded His disciples to "wash one another's feet", the way to titles and authority (John 13:5; 14).

Temperance (Self-control)

It is the Life of the Holy Spirit which gives us the ability to respond to every situation. It will enable you to be content in every situation. It teaches and disciplines the soul and causes it to be satisfied (Phil. 4:9-13). I can also say that I have truly experienced the feeling of being satisfied in challenging times.

Faith (Trust)

The Fruit of Faith

We need the fruit of faith to please God. It is the only attribute which enables us to live in the ways of His Spirit. God desires that we have complete trust and confidence in His power, totally leaning on Christ. Paul in his letter to the Colossians declares "we have heard of your faith in Messiah Yeshua", …that entire trust and confidence is in His power" (Col.1:3-4. CJB).

Fruits are the product of a union between either something or someone. The fruit of faith is the result of a union between the Holy Spirit with an individual. As we unite with Him the power of God is released; the evidence that He lives in us. His life can actively operate and flow as we are changed to reflect Christ in His fullness. Fruit grows from the branches of a tree and Christ is that Tree of Life. Though it has not been fully formed, however, during its development the fruit has the power to consistently remain a part of the tree. Life flows into the branches which receives food. Yeshua clearly presents this point when He declares that He is the vine and His Father is the Farmer. John 15:1 KJV. If we say that we live in Christ then we must show evidence of His attributes (fruit). If not, we are deceived and will eventually be destroyed (John 15:1-8).

In a careful study of Colossians 1:4-6, we learn that the fruits of the Spirit do work together. We see that the Colossians heard the Good News, which allowed them to understand the kindness (grace) of God and His plan for their lives. Paul refers to this grace in verses 5-6, as that which brought hope. Faith, which we can describe as 'deep settled', resulted from hope. They could now believe the message, and make a total surrender of their lives to the Messiah, with full confidence in His power, and wisdom.

We again say, that the fruit of the Spirit is evidence of the mighty indwelling power of God in us.

Paul, carefully analyses this process, by which the fruits of the Holy Spirit are cultivated in our lives. He explains that although each may carry its distinct quality, yet they are unified in operation. The evidence of this work is seen in us when we show the character of Christ; we become more like Him as we die to our desires (Galatians 4:19). Our Father's desire will become our sole focus until we can say "Father not my will but yours be done" (Luke 22:42 KJV).

AUTHORITY

- God (The Living Water) has chosen us

We see a picture of God's choice by the encounter of the Samaritan woman with Jesus at Jacob's well (John 4:7-26). It was at that place that Jesus revealed God to her as 'Father.' As a result, her identity, dignity, and self-worth were restored. Yeshua caused her to realise that she was God's daughter; upon this revelation of her new identity, she was able to see Him as her heavenly Father.

As we read further, Jesus reveals that the "water" v.13-14 which He offers is the Holy Spirit, who would live permanently within her and give a changed and purposeful life, with freedom and a new understanding to worship God. The woman now clearly understands that she can call God "Father" whom she once worshipped in ignorance. She can now tell the men in the city "come see a man......" (John 4:28-29. KJV).

Authority – God has called us Sons

On the last day of the Feast of Tabernacles, Jesus stood up and exclaimed, "if anyone is thirsty, let him keep coming to me and drink! Whoever puts his trust in me, as the Scripture says, rivers of living water will flow from his innermost being!" (John 7:37 CJB). He was referring to the Holy Spirit who was about to come. Paul writing to the Galatians declares that sons of God call Him "Father" because His Spirit lives in them (Galatians 4:6). Before God created the world, He chose us, filled us with His Holy Spirit, the Spirit of His Son, so that we in turn should become sons. The Father, Son, and Holy Spirit are one. The Hebrew word is "Echad." They work together as one (1 John 5: 7-8).

The scripture tells us that God commanded Moses that ancient Israel, on the same day that they came out of Egypt, should wait at the bottom of the mountain of Sinai in the wilderness. He was instructed to remind them of the blessings which they would receive if they were obedient and kept His covenant; that He would exalt them above all people, and they shall be unto Him "a kingdom of priests, and a holy nation." Exodus 19:1-6. They were not permitted to "...... go up into the mount" (v.12). However, when Jesus was about to return to His Father, He took three of His disciples with Him, Peter, James, and John, to the mount of transfiguration into the very presence of the Father's glory (Mark 9:2-3). He knew the heart of His Father, that they should become sons and heirs. After His resurrection, few could recognise Him. However, it was only after they had felt the scars in His hands and feet (Luke 24:39-40) and shared a meal at the Covenant Table (v.41-43), around which they had previously gathered, did they realise that He was truly their Lord!

OBEDIENCE

The main purpose of the Holy Spirit is to create the qualities of Yeshua in us, and transform us into sons of God. He uses the process of obedience as He did with His Son, Jesus.

"Let this mind be in you, which was also in Christ Jesus, who being in the form of God, thought it not robbery to be equal with God, but made himself of no reputation, and took unto himself the form of a servant, and was made in the likeness of men. And being found in fashion as a man, he humbled himself and became obedient unto death even the death of the cross. Wherefore God has highly exalted him, and given him a name which is above every name, that at the name of Jesus, every knee should bow, of things in heaven, and things in earth, and things under the earth; and that every tongue should confess that Jesus Christ is Lord to the glory of God the Father" (Philippians 2:4-11. KJV)

Yeshua put aside His Divinity, and came to us as a man in order to establish His title as "the only" and "First Begotten Son of God" on earth. He experienced the learning process of life, one which God used to develop full obedience to His will (Hebrews 1).

Obedience is one of the primary foundations upon which God's throne exists. Lucifer (also known as Satan after his downfall) gave up his right to be a son of God because of disobedience. We also learn that this was the reason which allowed Adam to lose his place in Eden. It was important that Yeshua should go through such a process which would result in great honour. The bible tells us that He learned obedience by the things He suffered.

During the days of Jesus' life on earth, He offered up prayers and petitions with loud cries and tears to the one who could save Him from death, and He was heard because of His relevant submission. Although

He was a Son, He learned "obedience from what He suffered" (Hebrews 5:7-9 NIV).

The effect of suffering is obedience. Yeshua humbled Himself to such an extent that He became completely submissive to His Father's will. The Holy Spirit may use situations which often result in seasons of difficulty and suffering. This He does, to mould us into His own sons and daughters. During this process, we learn to completely trust in God's wisdom as He works in our lives, and as sons we trust in His leading and guidance. "But as many as received Him, to them He gave the right to become children of God, even to those who believe in His name, who were born, not of blood, nor of the will of the flesh, nor of the will of man, but of God" (John 1:12-13 Ryrie Study Bible).

Note: Before the world had been created, the Father had chosen Yeshua to be His Son, however, His Sonship on earth could not have been established without Him having undergone the process of obedience. By this He established His honourable position as the first born Son of God, high above before all rulers, authorities, powers and dominion including every name which is invoked, not only in the present age but also in the one to come (Ephesians 1:17-21).

Being obedient to His Father's will was the crucial factor in the life of Yeshua. He is God, and always will be God, as such, He could have returned to His throne. However, He would forfeit the titles, Son of God, Messiah Yeshua, the perfect man, and Deliverer. He would not have fulfilled the righteousness of God which is obedience. Yeshua had to fulfil all that God required of every order of His created beings, by becoming the perfect example. It is important to understand that He was both God and man, divine and human. On earth His goal was to 'birth' sons and daughters for God.

We become Sons of God through obedience (John 1:12). We listen to His instructions and obey. The word 'become' suggests a process of change taking place in the lives of the sons of God. In Romans 8:14, Paul tells us "For all who are being led by the Spirit of God, these are sons of God." As a leader can only lead one who has made himself submissive, the Holy Spirit will lead only those who are obedient to His will. He gives instructions and reveals the Father's plans for our lives. As we learn to follow Gods desires, we discover His heart of obedience, as we begin to reflect His character, God sees His son being formed in us.

Prayer

> "Eternal Father of great wisdom, we stand in admiration of your Grace that you could open our minds and fill it with such understanding of your inner secrets. That which you concealed from the angelic beings, you now kindly reveal it unto us, "babes" young children. We honour You Heavenly Father, and You, our Lord and Big Brother, Yeshua. Wonderful Holy Spirit, may you continue to finish the awesome transforming work that you, even before we knew You, had already began in us; Holy Spirit, may you teach us diligently to be sons and daughters of The Father, to walk in His great house with kingly dignity and authority as sons even as Yeshua, our Elder Brother is; bringing great joy and honour and pleasure to you, Heavenly Father. May our lives also be an example to others that they may seek intently to become sons of God and enter into their eternal and personal inheritance that is reserved in heaven for all those whom you foreordained before the foundations of the world; thank you dear Father, in the honour of your First Son, Yeshua."

Obedience through the Holy Spirit

God said to His Son "I will proclaim the decree: Adonai said to me You are my son; today I have become your Father" (Psalms 2:7 CJB). As a result the Spirit of God was birthed into Yeshua who later became a man and exchanged His life for us. The next part of God's plan, to reveal in us His Holy Spirit, who is the Father of life. We are born of His Spirit and carry His name not as the angels who have been "created."

The role of the Holy Spirit is to develop the character of Jesus in our lives so that we may reflect that of the Father. We read in 2 Corinthians 3:18, "But we all, with unveiled face, beholding as in a mirror the glory of the Lord, are being transformed into the same image from glory to glory, just as from the Lord, the Spirit."

His Holy Life: The Greek word for life is "Pnuema." His Holy Spirit transforms us into His image from glory to glory.

The Greek word "Metamorphoo," means to change, transfigure and to "transform."

The image and Glory of God is the Man, Messiah Yeshua.

We have been chosen to hold the privileged position of a joint inheritance with the Messiah in God's eternal kingdom. Messiah Yeshua made intercession for us saying "The glory which you have given me I have given to them, that they may be one, just as we are one; I in them and You in me, that they may be perfected in unity, so that the world may know that You sent me, and loved them, even as you have loved me" (John 17:22-23).

THE POSITION OF KINGS

A very important declaration of truth I found in the above verse. "I have given them the Glory and the honour which you have given me." While we examine the statement, we can ask the question, "what glory and honour is Yeshua referring to?" He was referring to the glory and honour which was given to Him because of His relation to God His Father as His Son. He became the Father's first Son and heir to all His possessions. By the name Yeshua, He secured a rank superior to the Angels; Paul declares in Hebrews that it was 'different from' and 'more excellent than theirs' (Hebrews 1:5-14). The entire creation of spiritual beings were made subject to Him, for He had fulfilled His Father's plan for His life while on earth. In the book of Hebrews, Paul describes His role as 'Kingly' where we are reminded that a king rules while he sits on his throne. The angels (our brothers) are created beings; they hold different roles and offices of authority according to God's purposes; however, the Son inherits the official right to be King (Psalms 45: 6-7), (Heb.1: 2-9).

Yeshua acquired His kingly position through His BIRTHRIGHT which was sealed by the anointing of the Spirit of God, with much joy and gladness. Psalms 45:6-7. KJV (Hebrews 1:6 KJV; verse 8-10 KJV).

We as sons and fellow brothers, chosen before this world had been created, can confidently claim to be joint heirs with Yeshua our Messiah. This is the honour which Christ has given to us. It has always been the plan of God to mould us into the nature and character of His Son, allowing us to go through the processes of life designed to effect obedience in our lives just as Jesus Christ (1 Cor.2:12).

We, as mentioned before, had been chosen, called through His Holy Spirit, forgiven of our sins, and given right standing i.e. made righteous. Finally, we became glorified when He exalted us to a heavenly dignity!

We now sit in the spiritual realm by the Father's side and have become inheritors of all His possessions. We can fulfil the Father's will to give birth to sons and daughters.

THE UNVEILING ROLE OF THE HOLY SPIRIT

The prophet Ezekiel is receiving a revelation of the plan and purpose of God for man. One may dwell on the thought, that the Holy Spirit is allowing him to hear parts of a conversation which took place long before creation. "A new heart also will I give you and a new spirit will I put within you….and I will put my Spirit within you…moreover I will make an everlasting covenant with them…my tabernacle also shall be with them; yea I will be their God and they shall be my people" (Ezekiel 36:26-27 and 37:26-27). When the Eternal God had placed His own Spirit in us, He caused us to become Sons and we reflected His character and personality. In John 20:22, we read that Jesus "breathed on them and said receive ye the Holy Ghost." Now we say, 'Abba' meaning "Dear Father."

After they had received His Spirit, Yeshua instructs His disciples of the importance of faith and love for Him. He then makes this promise by saying, "If you really love me, keep (obey) my commandments (instructions) and I will ask the Father and He will give you another Comforter that He may remain with you forever even the Spirit of Truth whom the world cannot receive because it does not see, know or recognise Him. But you know and recognise Him for He lives with you and will be in you. I will not leave you as orphans; I will come to you" (John 14: 13-18 Amp. Bible).

The above scripture mentions the word 'another.' Yeshua does not refer to another being, but the very same Spirit and not a duplicate. The CJB translates this verse "and I will ask the Father and He will give you another comforting Counsellor like me, The Spirit of Truth, to be with you forever." Yeshua again says 'like me.' This is the same Spirit which the Eternal Father sent to the virgin Mary when she conceived Yeshua. We see later, after He was baptised, the Father affirmed His Son by declaring 'This is my beloved Son whom I love; I am well pleased with Him.' Before He was taken into Heaven, Yeshua promised His disciples that He would ask the Father to send them the same Spirit who had filled and empowered His life i.e. the Holy Spirit Greek word (Ruach Hakodesh). We read later in Mark 9:1-3, of Yeshua taking three of His disciples, Peter, James, and John up a high mountain. There they witnessed a great transformation, He changes His appearance, His clothes, 'everyday' and 'ordinary' become dazzling white. In amazement they watch and witness the prophets Moses and Elijah conversing with Yeshua and hear the voice of God, the Father. Despite their fear, they now have their personal testimony of the Messiah (the Anointed One).

This event takes place after He had mentioned that the Kingdom of God would come with power. We could ask the question "what did Jesus possibly mean?" He was revealing to them that God was about to send His Holy Spirit, to reside in man; they would be the first to experience His indwelling presence by His Grace and the exchange of His covenant.

When Yeshua had completed His ministry on earth, He prayed to His Father "I have given them the honour which you have given to me… I in them and you in me, in order that they may become one and perfectly united, that the world may know and (definitely) recognize that you sent me and that you have loved them (even) as you have loved me (John 17:4, 22-23 Amp. Bible).

The Apostle Paul declares "I live, yet not I, but Messiah Yeshua now lives in me." He is saying that it is the Spirit of Yeshua who is actively living His life in him, defining Grace as "God living in him."

Oh the depth of the riches of the love that our Heavenly Father has bestowed upon us who receive His Grace!

When God visits Abram in the plains of Mamre, we see a shadow of His heart and plan for man (Genesis 18: 1-5). Abram invites the "three men" to share a meal with him to which they have agreed. There we see God unveiling His plans; man having close fellowship with Him. He expresses these in two ways; first He places the "promise word" into the heart of Sarah; she disbelieves and laughs. We learn later in Genesis 18:17 that God shares His plans with Abraham "and the Lord said, shall I hide from Abraham (my friend and servant) what I AM GOING TO DO?" (Gen.18:17-18 Amp. Bible).

The Ultimate Goal of The Spirit
The ultimate goal of the Holy Spirit is to transform us into the image and likeness of Yeshua so that He may at the right time, present us to the Father. This plan can only be fulfilled by the New and everlasting covenant through Yeshua Messiah. The principle of covenant became the foundation for such a plan. After the fall of Adam, we see God covering their nakedness by making clothes from the skin of an animal (Gen.3:21). These coverings became a symbol of the covenant, an exchange, the death of an animal to cover the guilt of Adam. However, the perfect plan of God had been fulfilled through the death and resurrection of His Son, by which all received forgiveness and freedom! When the Father looked at the covering, He would remember the death of an innocent animal.

We read in Gen.7:14-18, when God saw the corruption on earth that the principle of covenant came into operation.

"Make thee an ark of gopher wood and behold I, even I, do bring a flood of waters upon the earth...but with thee will I establish my covenant."

Noah and his family had been protected in the ark. At the end of the storm, after one hundred and fifty days upon leaving the ark, Noah offered sacrifices of a sweet savour unto God and He again established His covenant between man and every living creature upon the earth. He placed a bow in the sky, as a symbol of covenant exchange, a promise to pour out abundant blessings through Grace (Gen. 9:8-17 Amp. Bible).

To obey the will of His Father on earth was an important factor in the life of Yeshua; the salvation of man and the Sovereign Authority of the Godhead remained dependant on His actions. To truly understand this statement, we must look into John's gospel which focuses on the humanity, and divinity of Christ. In John 17:1, we read "Jesus spoke these things: and lifting up His eyes to heaven, He said, Father, the hour has come: glorify your Son that the Son may glorify you." Yeshua was not making a petition to His Father but He was making two declarations of truth, firstly, His identity, and secondly, His position in the Godhead according to the master plan. If one would ask the question "how would the Father glorify the Son Yeshua?" I believe that both His statement and request had wider implications than His death and resurrection on the cross.

THE DECLARATION

When Yeshua made the statement 'glorify your son', He had already been glorified in the heavenly realms from the moment that God desired to give birth to an earthly Son who in turn would give birth to many sons and daughters. When He declared in Psalms 2:7 "I will surely tell of the decree of the Lord, He said to me you are my Son, today I have begotten you" (Ryrie Study Bible). At this time, God glorified, lifted up, and granted honour to His Son by crediting His reputation above every other created being. The mark of distinction demanded the absolute reverence of all beings because of His superior position. A human body was prepared for Yeshua and upon entering He had to learn the disciplines of obedience even unto the point of death, throughout His developmental stages of childhood to that of a young man. He pleased the Father who proudly declared 'This is my beloved Son in whom I am well pleased' (Mark 9:7 KJV). This joyful declaration was to be heard throughout every spiritual domain. It authenticated and endorsed glory, and honour to God's Son, Jesus; the Messiah-King which, of course, was His inherent right. In addition, this declaration showed that Jesus' action of total submission within the context of His earthly role, proved His love for His Father. Jesus having earned the right to do so, stood in absolute righteousness of obedience before all the orders of created beings and, in particular, Satan, and those angels who fell with him. God's declaration prevented accusations in regard to the Lordship of Yeshua, God's Son over them.

As this authority is given by the favour of inheritance, Yeshua continues to say '....that the Son also may glorify thee.' Here it is important to notice that He is not speaking in the first person singular "me" but He speaks about himself using the third person plural "your Son" as though He is referring to someone else, yet we are clear that He is speaking about

Himself. At this point, He looks into the spiritual realm, and sees the eternal plan which God had made before creation. By making this declaration, one could say that He reminded the Father of their relationship and His perfect plan to give birth to a Son and NOT a created being.

Yeshua continues to declare **"I have completed the work that you gave me to do."**

"Can you imagine what the declaration meant to the Godhead in heaven? From the moment He was conceived in the mind of the Eternal God, "…..In the volume of the book, (in the depth of God's heart) it is written of me" (Psalm 40:7 KJV), until the time that the Father activated the second stage of the birth of His Son, sealing the entrance with the words "This day I have begotten thee," (Psalm 2:7) proceeding from His physical birth at Bethlehem, and culminating at the hour of His death at Calvary, His Father waited with "bated breath" to hear this astounding declaration!

None of the created beings has ever been able to make such a declaration, which would entail total obedience to God's sovereign authority, not Satan though created as a "son" and was positioned as an "anointed cherub which covered the throne of God" (Ezekiel 28:14). Is it any wonder that his attack on Yeshua in the wilderness was intent on releasing and tempting His authority to perform miracles as God, and not within His role as Man. In this capacity, He would be wholly dependent on His Father. Had Yeshua been enticed by this devious suggestion to rely on His divinity and power, Satan would have the legal right to quash all claims of His authority over him. He would have gained the victory over the claims of God, that no being either created or born would ever be obedient to His commands.

One could imagine Satan's constant taunts on Yeshua during the wilderness as:

'if you are the Son of God…..perform these miracles.'

'If you are from eternity, and if you say you are God then do these things.'

'Come away from your humanity.'

'Take back your divinity…because as God you are not subject to obedience.'

However, Yeshua quoted the Word from the beginning "It is written I am under subjection to what God has said: I am a "man" under OBEDIENCE and I am a Son under OBEDIENCE to my Father's commandments. I have put aside my equality with God. I have humbled myself, and I am a servant!" Only the man, Messiah Yeshua, the Anointed One who came from God could make such a statement in loving obedience to the Father.

As a result of obedience to His Father's commandments, He triumphantly declared, "I have finished the work!" proving to all principalities, powers, and rulers of all dispensations and domains that the Authority of God is righteous, and His commandments are just. The heavenly angelic beings could only look on in amazement and watch this mystery, not yet revealed, but now being unveiled before their very eyes.

The obedience of Yeshua has given Him the rights of Lordship, having both initiated and established God's law of obedience. This act now crowns Him as Lord, and proves that His word is faithful, and God in His essence, is the completion of obedience. Every created being can now honour and obey Jesus, the Son of God, as the one who has earned the right of worship, because of His obedience.

If we look at the next section of the verse we read .."**the work you gave me to do" (John 17:4).** Here, in Yeshua's report we see a clear picture of agreement in the completion of this eternal Master Plan, first seen in the opening picture of God's creation in Genesis 1. The Spirit working together as God speaks His Word, and His Spirit hovers over the vast waters during creation. Later in John 1, he begins his opening line by saying 'In the beginning was the Word', 'the Word was with God', 'the

Word was God.' Again we see a work of unity (1 John 5:7). The word 'work' implies the stage or part of the plan where the Son comes to live as a man. This assignment was fundamentally important to the Sovereignty of God, His integrity, and the "salvation" of man, as sons born of God.

SPIRITUAL CREATIONS

Earlier, I used the word 'mystery' when describing the angels as they watched the unravelling of the plan. What was this 'mystery?' To understand it, we must find a 'thread' which is both undeniable, and evident throughout the entire bible. It is a declaration made by God in which we see the continuation of the creation of all His spiritual beings in their specific forms e.g. Angels and the 'living beings.' When He unfolded His great master plan, it consisted of spirit beings called Angels or Messengers, and human beings who are body, soul, and spirit. The universal principle to secure their existence was obedience to God's authority. It was God's desire that such obedience to this authority by His created beings would be by their own volition, and without pressure because of the experience of His unending love and power. By observing this principle, they would function in alignment with God's eternal plan. The Eternal Life, given to humans, represented in Eden as the Tree of Life, by which Adam would have gained eternal life, and not death, had he obeyed.

There are two types of obedience; one is the result of constraint e.g. the type demanded by one in authority with the result of an inward unwilling response. The second type can be compared to the Father and His Sons. God, in His wisdom, foresaw the rebellion of the angels, and the disobedience of man. He knew that the absolute authority could only be initiated, and established, only through Himself as "the role model." This concept may be difficult to understand, however we must remember that He is God, and His ways and thoughts are different to us. He created us! He initiated a master plan, which would become the mystery of the ages! "Have this attitude in yourselves which was also in Christ Jesus, who, although He existed in the form of God, did not regard equality with God a thing to be grasped, but emptied Himself, taking the form of a bond-servant, and being made in likeness of men" (Philippians 2:5-7. Ryrie Study Bible).

When Yeshua came in human form, He humbled himself even further by becoming obedient to death! Not just a natural death but a horrific, torturous death on a stake (cross). However, His Father gave Him the highest position of authority, and the greatest name. Yeshua (Salvation) as written in the book of Ephesians, that every human, and spiritual being will give Him the highest honour to His name, and every person will declare that Yeshua the Messiah is Lord, to the glory of God the Father!

During His life on earth, His communication with His Father was sometimes made whilst crying aloud as He prayed earnestly, and appealed to Him on our behalf. He prayed to the only One who had the power to save Him from death. The bible tells us that He was heard because of His godliness. Though He was a Son, He learned obedience through the things He suffered, and was later "proclaimed by God as a High Priest to be compared with Melchizedek" (Hebrews 5:7-9, Phil. 2:5-11). Only then was He able to rescue those who listen to His teachings, and obey them.

In His teachings on the Mount of Olives, Yeshua brought the Spirit of Life to the instructions which were first given by God to Moses. These were heard, and received by those who believed. He warned the people about the dangers of false teachers, and as a true test, instructed them to observe characters and actions before establishing whether these teachers were true or fake. Jesus compared people to trees, the healthy ones would produce good fruits while others bad fruit. He implied that fruit (actions, character) reveal the true condition of the tree (person). He continued to state that not everyone who called Him 'Lord' would enter His Kingdom but only those who obey His Father's instructions. He explained that there would be a time ("that day") when many people would cry out to Him saying that the actions they performed such as driving out demon spirits, and other outstanding acts were done in His name. However, His Father would publicly reject them as their activities were wicked i.e. they had not obeyed His commands (Matt. 7:21-23). Later, Jesus speaks plainly to His disciples, and explains that **obedience to His Father's commands is what He accepts and not our miraculous accomplishments!**

Affirming this truth, Yeshua tells His disciples that the one who walks in obedience to the Father's will is wise, and his life is secured on the Rock. That person's life is then unmoveable as they walk in obedience to the will of God.

In this position of obedience, one can sustain the attacks from evil spirits and, in the event of a fall, will rise because of an established life based on the truth of God's word, and acts of obedience. Without this behaviour in an ever changing world, life would be useless and subject to failure.

Obedience to God is vital for such he will recognise as faith, just as the air we breathe. The Apostle James says that faith without actions is dead faith. This means that faith without obedience to the Word is lifeless because obedience to God's instructions allows faith to come alive and gives honour to his integrity. James explains "For as the body without the spirit is dead, so faith without (obedience) works is dead also" (James 2:17-26 KJV).

OBSERVING THE TEMPLE RULES FOR VERIFYING A HEALING

When Yeshua had finished teaching on the mountain, He came down, and was followed by a large crowd. Immediately He was met by a man with leprosy who knelt before Him, and appealed for healing. The man was healed, however Yeshua requested that He remain silent until, in accordance with Jewish law, he had shown his body to the temple priest, and offer pigeons as the expected sacrificial offering. Only then could his healing be verified. Jesus understood the Rabbinic legal regulations of this act, and agreed with those aspects of Temple service which were good, and served the people. However, He **challenged those binding laws which sought to add and change the laws of God (Matt. 8:1-4).**

Soldier's Obedience

When a conversation about paying taxes arose, Jesus instructed His disciples to honour both the local authority (when it did not dishonour God) and God. Something even more significant happens which reinforces the point of Yeshua's obedience; it brings into perspective a deeper understanding of the instructions which He gave earlier to the people.

He visits Capernaum where He is met by a Roman army officer. He approaches Him pleading for the healing of a member of staff who is paralysed, and in intense pain at home. On hearing his plight, Yeshua offers to visit and heal the man. Amazingly, the officer tells Him to simply speak the word, and his boy would be healed. He explained further that he understood authority; not only was he under Roman authority but also led an army (Matt: 8:9). Yeshua was amazed at this level of trust, and exclaimed to those around that He had never found in Israel such faith as in someone who was non-Jewish (Matt.8:10). He revealed that many non-Jewish believers would come into the Kingdom to share in the full inheritance, (Ephesians 2:6), while those Jews who had disbelieved would miss out resulting in weeping (Matt.8:11-12). The request of the Roman soldier had been granted the moment Yeshua spoke words of healing.

This is an outstanding contrast between the non Jewish soldier, without any knowledge of the Torah (1st five books); The Writings (Psalms) and The Prophets. However, he understood that this Rabbi (Jewish teacher) had authority which surpassed that of Rome. Firstly, the soldier made the profound statement declaring his unworthiness to have Yeshua at his home, and secondly, by making this acknowledgement, he submitted to the authority of the words of Yeshua as the only source of divine healing. This was a revelation of Yeshua as a Son in relation to His Father. If I could rephrase the words of the officer, it would read: "I recognise that you are Lord over all things and in order for this to be true, you have had to learn the "disciplines" of obedience in God's kingdom. Therefore you have been given authority over people, spirits, and all things, "as well as this sickness."

Suffering
Yeshua, having experienced suffering, understood the important work which it achieves in our lives. In particular, the battle of the human will coupled with the painful struggles which constantly fight against that of the Father. As such, Yeshua recognised the degree to which the Roman soldier had learned obedience; he saw, and understood his heart. This tells us that the Father is honoured when we are disciplined, and through obedience, we are brought to a place of total submission to His will and purpose. **Faith walks with obedience**. The apostle James tells us "you see how that by works (obedience) a man is justified, and not by faith (simply

receiving the word as from God) only" (James 2:22-24 KJV). Today, as we hear His words, we must act in faith and obey because "Obedience is better than sacrifice and to hearken and do the Father's command is better than the fat offerings of good deeds" (1 Sam. 15:22). Whilst standing at the bottom of the mountain, the Israelites heard the words of God as spoken by Moses, and responded by saying "all that the LORD has spoken we will do!" Exodus 19:8. This could only be done through the power of God's Holy Spirit, and forgiveness through the shedding of the blood of Christ.

YESHUA AND THE FATHER ARE ONE

The apostle John tells us that, from the beginning, the Word was with God (John 1:1). The Glory which God had in the beginning was shared with His Son. The Father, and His Son exist equally, and are co-equal in power, and possession. There is only one exception, and that is in form. This was a temporary arrangement in order that Yeshua should live in a human body, until this stage in God's master plan had been completed. He is the exact image of God. We read in Philippians 2:6 that Yeshua did not wish to be equal with God as it is His inherent right. Jesus said to His disciples that if they had seen Him then they had seen His Father (John 14:9).

We see in the book of Philippians that Yeshua humbled Himself on two occasions: firstly in His divinity by taking on a human body, and secondly, in His humanity by submitting to the power of death. When He enters this world, He has already emptied Himself of the glory, power, and divinity, to such an extent that His divinity was veiled. He was acknowledged as God by Peter, and later by James and John as their relationship grew. Yeshua asks "who do men (people) say that I am Peter? Who do you say that the Son of Man is? And they said some say John the Baptist; and others Elijah; but still others Jeremiah, or one of the prophets." He said to them who do you say that I am? Simon Peter answered "You are the Christ, the Son of the living God" (Matt.16:13-16 KJV).

The Father, His Son, and Spirit are co-equal. Yeshua's title is Lord, signifying His work on earth, but His inherent nature is God. The title of "Lord" (Psalms 110) was given to Him by God His Father because He became the "author" of obedience, however, He gained this honour only as a result of humbling Himself to the point of death in order to fulfil the plan of His Father.

THE AUTHORITY AND OBEDIENCE OF CHRIST

In Philippians Chapter 2, we gain a brief insight into the eternal plan of God. In order to gain a better understanding of such, we can imagine (as detailed earlier in this book) that a meeting had taken place in God's great throne room between Himself, The Godhead. Let us remember that Yeshua had been killed before the world existed. The purpose of this discussion was to reveal God's plan for the creation of a Universe, a world which would inhabit two forms of living beings.

1. Spiritual beings called Angels
2. Another type of spirit being called "mankind" which would have a living soul, and "housed" in a body.

In this plan, authority is **represented by the Father;** however without obedience authority cannot be established in the world, as these walk together. God had to find obedience in the world. As stated above, two forms of living beings had been created, the angels who are spirits, and another form, having a living soul, and dwelling in a physical body called "mankind." God being Omniscient foresaw the angelic rebellion and the fall of man. Rebellion originated from the heart of a created son called Lucifer, **therefore obedience must now be established from a Son who has been born of God.**

Based on this knowledge, it was not possible for the Father to establish His authority through the total obedience of angelic beings, or the Adamic race. Christ though holding the authority as God, would not have experienced the loving obedience of His created beings. Therefore

He enters the human race with all its ramifications and becomes a servant in order to model authority.

There are two ways in which Yeshua was able to return to His kingdom. Firstly, through absolute obedience, and without reservation to His father. We remember the crucial point which led Him to obedience to the will of His Father. The bible tells us that "though He was a Son, yet learned He obedience through the things He suffered" (Hebrews 5:8 KJV). The second would have been by enforcing His rights as a deity, and reclaiming His position as God with authority and glory. However, He fulfilled this role within the limitations of a human body. "A body has thou prepared me, Then said I, Lo I come. In the volume of the book, it is written of me, to do thy will Oh God" (Psalm 40:7-8 KJV).

We cannot imagine the extent of the horrific consequences on the Godhead and over all creation, had Yeshua not upheld such a decision. However, our Messiah, Yeshua willingly submitted to the disciplines of obedience, and overcame the Adversary's deception which would allow Him to deviate from the Master Plan of God. We reflect on the judgement passed by God on Adam because of disobedience. This resulted in his fall in Eden. Immediately after judgement had been passed, we read that Cherubim were commanded to guard the entrance to the Tree of Life denying access to him. He lost his way to eternal life because of rebellion and disobedience! Both Adam and his wife are now living outside the Garden; the life originally created for them by God (Gen.3: 21-24).

Through obedience, Yeshua was able to overcome the devil. He was in total submission to the will of God, and His Word (Matthew 4:1-11). The fall of Adam and Eve in the Garden of Eden resulted as an Act of disobedience (Gen.3:3-13). However, the scriptures tell us that "he was in all points tempted like as we are, yet without sin" (Hebrews 4:15 KJ). He won total victory over the devil and made it possible for His sons to sit with Him on His throne, just as He now sits with His Father on His throne (Rev.3:21).

Jeshua was the perfect example to all who have His spirit, showing us that obedience is simply **submitting to God's will and His Spirit who gives us the power to live this life and extend His Kingdom here on earth.**

The Road to obedience – Sufferings and Honour

The apostle Paul in his passion to comprehend and experience the triumphant power of obedience, committed himself to know Christ by walking the road of suffering. He understood the ways in which the Holy Spirit used the hardships of life, "the light afflictions" to teach obedience. He allowed His own will to "die" that the will of the Father could be accomplished. The Messiah's Anointing, the Holy Spirit (Ruach HaKodesh) now lives in us; we have the ability to submit disciplines (note plural) of obedience. These teachings will enable us to be 'like Christ' and mirror His description by the Roman Soldier as "a man under authority." This is a model of a true Son of God affirmed by the Father as He did for Yeshua at His baptism when He declared "this is my beloved Son in whom I am well pleased" (Matthew 17:5 KJV).

"For we which live are always delivered unto death for Jesus sake, that the life also of Jesus might be made manifest in our flesh" (2 Corin. 4:11 KJV).

"He who overcomes, I will grant to him to sit down with me on my throne as I also overcame and sat down with my Father on His throne" (Revelation 3:21 KJV).

For Yeshua the disciplines of obedience were more challenging than creating the heavens and earth. Why? Because He had put aside all the glory and power of being the Eternal and Omnipotent God in order to become human and serve others. He had learned to be obedient and was able to endure the full force of the powers of disobedience; as a man, the second Adam, He triumphed over them. Through obedience, He earned the right to God's bright presence, the distinctive mark which distinguished Him as the "true" Son of God. His death on the cross was the ultimate submission to the disciplines of obedience, an act which established four things:

1. Demonstrated that truly He is the Son of God. Luke 23:46
2. Conquered the powers of darkness for all times. Col. 2:15
3. Restored and established order in the heavenly realms. Eph. 1:21-23
4. Guaranteed our eternal salvation. Heb. 5:8-9.

The sufferings of Christ secured the place of the highest distinction above all beings ever created, and have crowned us with glory and privilege. This knowledge is amazing. When our Messiah spoke about "emptying himself" (Philippians 2:7), He was refilled by God, His father, and restored to His glory; God the Son now becomes Yeshua the man. This sets His name, Jesus The Christ (Yeshua Ha'Mashiach) as most precious, and there is no one in the universe like Him. Hanging on the cross, He declared triumphantly; "it is finished" (John 19:30) proclaiming not only the accomplishment of salvation, but also the completion of all that His name and titles signify. Such and many more are the crowns of His glory.

"Therefore He had obtained a name, which is above every other name and at His name every knee shall bow, and every tongue shall confess that Yeshua is Lord" (Phil 2:9-11 KJV).

"Next I saw heaven opened, and there before me was a white horse. Sitting on it was the one called Faithful and True, and it is in righteousness that e passes judgment and goes to battle. His eyes were like a fiery flame and on his head were many royal crowns" (Revelation 19:11 CJB).

This prime example of total submission, reverence and confession, establishes that **Jesus is Lord and He is God!**

THE MIND OF THE MESSIAH

Because we are His sons, our heavenly Father (Abba) has given us the mind of His Son so that we, as sons, may reflect His characteristics and fulfil His amazing plans and purposes in our lives. The Holy Spirit (Ruach HaKodesh) who lives in us has given us the mind of Christ. This is not the pattern of His mental thought or every day thinking, but the different ways, intention and passion in which Yeshua served His Father even to His death.

We have the mind of Yeshua and are able to operate in obedience to His will; we now have the determination to fulfil His desires, whatever it may cost. The Apostle Paul in his passion to have the full experience of the mind of Christ, declares "Oh, that I may know Him, and the power of His resurrection, and the fellowship of His sufferings, and be made conformable unto His death" (Phil. 3:10. KJV).

Through this deep understanding, it was revealed to Paul that the Spirit living in him was the very essence of the Messiah and as such, he could think as Christ. This was not the type of thought which supported religious practices, however, one which would give the ability to be familiar with the thoughts of Christ; the experience of living the full life of Christ who had learned the disciplines of obedience. This level of trust enabled Paul to endure the bitter challenges of life, persecution, hardship, joy, plenty, little, friendships, loneliness, betrayal, judgement, and much more, even unto his death.

When we read the book of Matthew we see where Jesus made this profound statement "the disciple is not above his master, nor the servant above his Lord. It is enough for the disciple that he be as his master, and the servant as his Lord." Matt. 10:24 KJV. He taught that as His servants we should emulate Him; follow Him as our example. He gave us the pattern for living a victorious life here on earth. We can follow Him, and overcome every conflict and be called "trees of righteousness" (Isaiah 61:3). On another occasion, as He spoke to His disciples, He said "if any man serve me let him follow me" (John 12:26 KJV). He said to Peter "………follow me" (John 21:19 KJV).

The Holy Spirit /The Ruach Hakodesh
The promised 'pouring out' of the Holy Spirit (The Ruach), a life filled with power, which resurrected Yeshua from the dead. It was the powerful work operating in the lives of the disciples as outlined in the book of 'Acts.' It is the role of the Spirit to duplicate the nature and passion of service needed to fulfil the Father's plans for the extension of His Kingdom here on earth. This work enables us to serve God's people.

Our human spirits become alive to the Father as we allow Him to fill us with His life. We then receive the mind of the Messiah which enables us to think as a Son of God. This work will be the result of perfection in our spirits; causing us to develop an attitude of service, a lifestyle portraying the characteristics of Sons of God. These events have been planned to take place, according to the original design implanted in us at the time of our creation in Eden. The character of Jesus came from a pure and righteous heart which allowed Him to show deep emotion of compassion for human suffering. The mind of Christ will enable us to operate as He did, with His God character. Such qualities must be seen at home, among friends, the greater family of believers, in our local communities, in all places where we function.

In his letter to the Philippians, Paul makes the appeal to think like Yeshua. In this translation, the word at the beginning of the sentence is "let" (Phil.2:5 KJV) which directs our attention to the most crucial element for a lifestyle pointing to that of Yeshua. He emphatically declares to the Corinthians that we have the mind of the Messiah, the divine understanding, cognitive functioning, and Godly compassion. We are now able to give up our plans in exchange for God's own purposes for our lives.

The Apostle Paul declares "For who have known the mind of the Lord that he may instruct him, but we have the mind of the Messiah" (1 Cor: 2:16).

The Greek word for mind is Nous (Nooce). It refers to the intellect, i.e. the mind (divine or human, in thought, feeling, or will): By implication meaning - mind, understanding.

When we have the mind of the Messiah and operate in it, our relationship with the Father will be radically transformed, and we will always choose to spontaneously obey His instructions without question but rather saying, "Father,...... not my will be done, but yours be done" (Luke 22:42 NIV).

When the Holy Spirit referred to the mind and attitude of Yeshua concerning the will of His Father, He declared, "Then said I, Lo, I come in the volume of the book it is written of me (in the scroll of the book it is written of me) to do Thy will, Oh God (Heb.10:7 KJV). We must recall that this conversation took place before the world began; in eternity past. Making this statement was not a referral to written scripture, but to the Father's all knowing heart that His Son, through the power of His spirit, would carry out His will.

As we read the word of God, we learn that He has good plans for our lives, and has given us the same Holy Spirit which enables us to fulfil them. We are very familiar, and often quote the words of Jeremiah the Prophet, where God reveals His good plans for us "For I know what plans I have in mind for you, says Adonai, plans for well-being, not for bad things, so that you can have hope and a future. When you seek me you will find me, provided you seek for me wholeheartedly, and I will let you find me, says

Adonai. Then I will reverse your exile, I will gather you from all nations and place where I have driven you, says Adonai, and bring you back to the place from which I exiled you" (Jeremiah 29:11-14 CJB).

His perfect plans are to raise us up from the dead and set us at His own right hand in the heavenly places far above all principalities, powers, might and dominion, and every name that is named, not only in this world, but also that which is to come (Eph. 1:20-21).

This is a gift of God who is rich in mercy towards us, to the extent that when we were dead in sins, He had never ceased to love us! Even when we were dead in sins, through the same Spirit (Ruach) in Messiah Yeshua, God has brought our spirits back to life as He did for His Son. Ephesians declares that we are saved through grace and not by our good works, but the gift of God (Eph.2:4-8). "Not of works, lest any man should boast" verse 9.

It is the plan of the Father that we, His family, should walk with kingly dignity in the presence of angels and men. Hallelujah! Let the mind of Christ allow us to walk as His sons with humble hearts and an attitude of obedience. Let our will die so that His planned will may become alive in us.

The apostle Paul states confidently that we have the mind of the Messiah. We have been fully equipped to

1. Function as Sons in our environment
2. Supernaturally empowered through the Spirit of Yeshua to demonstrate every virtue unique to a Son of God.

We have received the mind of the Holy Spirit which is the Spirit and mind of Jesus; this enables us to be conformed to the image of Christ. This ongoing work helps us to live the life of the Messiah as the revealed sons of God, which the whole of creation is expectantly awaiting.

THE REVEALED SONS OF GOD

The Apostle Paul when he reveals the mystery of the plan of God for all generations, gives a snippet of the overall picture (Romans 8:14-25 CJB).

"All who are led by God's Spirit are God's sons. For you did not receive a spirit of slavery to bring you back again into fear, on the contrary, you received the Spirit, who makes us sons and by whose power we cry out "Abba" (that is "Dear Father"). The Spirit Himself bears witness with our own spirits that we are children of God, and if we are children, then we are suffering with him in order also to be glorified with him. I don't think the sufferings we are going though now are even worth comparing with the glory that will be revealed to us in the future. The creation waits eagerly for the sons of God to be revealed for the creation was made subject to frustration - not willingly, but because of the one who subjected it. But it was given a reliable hope that it too would be set free from its bondage to decay and would enjoy the freedom accompanying the glory that God's children will have. We know that until now, the whole creation has been groaning as with the pains of childbirth, and not only it, but we ourselves, who have the first fruits of the spirit, groan inwardly as we continue waiting eagerly to be made sons - that is, to have our whole bodies redeemed and set free. It was in this hope that we were saved. But if we see what we hope for, it isn't hope - after all, who hopes for what he already sees? But if we continue hoping for something we don't see, then we still wait eagerly for it, with perseverance."

Paul states that all creation is eagerly waiting for the sons of God to be revealed. Because of Adam's disobedience in Eden, the ground was made subject to the curse "Because you have listened to the voice of your wife, and have eaten from the tree about which I commanded you, saying you shall not eat from it, cursed is the ground because of you: in toil you will eat of it all the days of your life. Both thorns and thistles it shall grow for you and you will eat of the plants of the field, by the sweat of your face you will eat bread, till you return to the ground because from it you were taken for you are dust, and to dust you shall return" (Genesis 3:17-19 Ryrie Study Bible).

Today it is evident that the whole creation is suffering from the catastrophic events taking place; global climatic changes, hurricanes, tsunamis, earthquakes, famines, drought, and diseases. There are many more which could be added. Such are examples and evidence of the sufferings of the earth, coupled with its cries to the Creator against the immeasurable amount of human blood which it receives on a daily basis.

Despite such effects on earth, God, the great architect, in accordance with His plan by which His grace would be revealed, through a word of Covenant with Himself, that the earth would eventually be delivered from this bondage of corruption; and be transformed to its former glory where His people could live. It would again be God's tithe, from His creation, a first fruit unto Himself, His Eden of delight. The earth would undergo a process, as it were "a metamorphism" emerging from darkness to light, from death to life, when the sons and daughters of God will celebrate its new life with its creator, Yeshua Messiah, the Son of God.

Our Bodies

When Paul wrote to the believers in Corinth, he drew their attention to the mystery of God's plan for their physical bodies. He gave an account of numerous incidences given by his disciples of the death, burial and resurrection of Yeshua. He continued to speak of his own miraculous story of his encounter with the Messiah while on the road to Damascus.

Having described these credible accounts as reliable proof of the Messiah, he then denounces the current false teachings saying "Now if Christ is preached, that He has been raised from the dead, how do some among you say that there is no resurrection of the dead? But if there is no resurrection of the dead, not even Christ has been raised: and if Christ has not been raised, then our preaching is vain, your faith also is vain. Moreover we are even found to be false witnesses of God, because we testified against God that he raised Christ, whom he did not raise, if infact the dead are not raised. For if the dead are not raised, not even Christ has been raised, and if Christ has not been raised, your faith is worthless, you are still in your sins. Then those also who have fallen asleep in Christ had perished. If we have hoped in Christ in this life only, we are all men most to be pitied" (1 Corinthians 15:12-19 The Ryrie Study Bible).

In other words, if the Messiah did not rise from the dead, the Covenant which God had made with His Son when He promised that He would not leave His soul in Hades, the grave (holding place for the dead) the result would be a broken covenant and our hope of a new Creation would have been crushed. However, Messiah has risen from the dead (Hallelujah) and has become the first fruits of them that sleep. "For since by man came death, even by man came also the resurrection of the dead. For as in Adam all die, even so in Christ shall all be made alive" (1 Corin.15:21-22 Thompson CHAIN REFERENCE BIBLE).

In the true cultural style of Hebrew debate, Paul anticipates possible questions e.g. "How do dead people come back to life? What body will they have?" Paul draws on a simple analogy of the growth of a seed. He explains that the plant is different to the seed when it is first planted into the ground. It is God who chooses the type of "body." He gives further examples of humans, spirits and animals, they are all different, however, created to adapt to their environment. He speaks of the beauty of the sun in contrast to the beauty of the moon and stars, though different, yet magnificent! He supports his statement by outlining this principle. Paul boldly states after our bodies have been raised from their graves they will be beautiful and glorious and never age. There are bodies which belong to heaven and those which belong to earth. The splendour of the heavenly bodies is different to the earthly bodies.

He states further that Adam, who was the first man, was made a physical being, however, the last Adam became a life giving spirit (1 Corin. 15:45). The first principle teaches that the natural life came first, and not the spiritual. Adam was made from the earth, however, the second Adam, Yeshua came from heaven. Paul concludes by saying as we have been made from the earth, we will eventually be made with a spiritual body (verse 44). We cannot gain access to the spiritual realm in a limited human body. These bodies have not been given the capacity to live forever, or travel through time and space. However, our new bodies will be like Yeshua's when He appeared to His disciples after His resurrection. He destroyed the power of death over the old body.

Paul added to this encouraging revelation, stating that some of us will not die but will miraculously, and instantly have new bodies to take us through the next stage of our journey! At the sound of the last trumpet those who have died in Messiah Yeshua will instantly come back to life in new bodies, and never experience death. Those who are alive will also be transformed into new bodies. "Thanks be to God, the victory is ours through our Lord Yeshua our Messiah" (1 Corinthian: 15). We will be changed from one glorious state to another to reveal God's face, and unlike Moses, the brilliant radiance of this change will involve not just our faces, but the whole body. This will be an everlasting triumph over Satan and his associates throughout eternity. It will reinforce to the hierarchical evil spirits that Christ alone is Omnipotent and He is MORE THAN ABLE to accomplish His plans!

Death, Suffering and Hope

Paul identified the feelings of despair when confronted with questions as we look at our bodies or those of our loved ones suffering from debilitating illness or trauma. These bodies will eventually die, however, they will be brought back to life in the same way that God did with Jesus. If you have lost a loved one, be encouraged for you will see them again in powerful, spiritual, and radiant new bodies. "...for this we declare to you by the Lord's word, that we who are alive and remain until the coming of the Lord shall in no way proceed into His presence or have any advantage at all over those who have previously fallen asleep. For the Lord Himself will descend from heaven with a loud cry of summons, with the shout of an archangel and with the blast of the trumpet of God. And those who have departed this life in Yeshua the Messiah will rise first.

Then we the living ones who remain on the earth shall simultaneously be caught up along with the resurrected dead in the clouds to meet the Lord in the air, and so always and eternally be with the Lord! Therefore comfort and encourage one another with these words" (1 Thess. 4:13-18 Amp.Bible).

Paul makes us aware that the lives of the believers who have died, would be preserved though they had not seen the promise made concerning Jesus (Hebrews 11:13). He states clearly that they were firmly grounded in their faith and as such, expanded the Kingdom of God through their different spiritual gifts and talents, having been made aware of their temporary existence on earth. However, if they did not believe that there was hope for an eternal future, they would have focussed on returning to their everyday lives. Paul further states that for this reason God is proud to be called their God. "But now, they desire a better country, that is, a heavenly, wherefore God is not ashamed to be called their God, for he has prepared for them a city" (Hebrews 11:16.KJV).

Beloved, we shall be like Him; for this is His inheritance in us ….this is the manifestation of the essence of His Covenant.

SATAN THE ADVERSARY

The Apostle Paul explains "we were by nature the children of wrath (God's) and heirs of (His) indignation, like the rest of mankind" (Ephesians 2:3-5). Satan knew that the nature of God is holiness and His demands are just; with great cunning He choreographed the downfall of man by using Adam and Eve in Eden. He knew that the impact of this decision would have resulted in their destruction and the fulfilment of God's words. He anticipated that God would destroy His First Fruit; the creation which would reflect His glory. However, the Father knew that the intent and purpose of the plan of His adversary was to deprive Him of His eternal glory and the rich satisfaction of His glorious inheritance in His family which He had set aside for Himself.

To think that the Eternal God would end His creation is quite unimaginable, however, Satan failed in his attempt. He did not understand the many sided wisdom of the Eternal God and failed to perceive His intense love for His family. (In His love) He chose us (actually picked us out for Himself as His own) in the Messiah before the foundation of the world, (that we should be holy, consecrated and set apart for Him) and blameless in His sight even above reproach before Him in love. "For I always pray to the God of our Lord Yeshua our Messiah, the Father of glory, that He may grant you a spirit of wisdom and revelation (of insight into mysteries and secrets) in the (deep and intimate) knowledge of Him. By having the eyes of your heart flooded with light, so that you can know and understand the hope to which He has called you, and how rich is His glorious inheritance in the saints (His set apart ones)" (Eph.1:4; 17, 18 Amp Bible).

Yes the righteous and powerful God would be justified if He had inflicted punishment on us. However, because of His intense love for His family, and the riches of His grace and mercy we have been pardoned. Before the world had been created He chose His Son to die in our place. The life of the Messiah was given in exchange for our broken lives and we have been delivered. We now have been raised into a new life with Jesus and rest with Him in the Heavenly sphere. He did this in order to reveal in the coming ages, His free undeserving grace, which can be seen in the kindness and goodness of His heart.

But God, so rich in His mercy! Collins Dictionary states: Mercy (noun) compassion: refraining from infliction of suffering by one who has right (and) power to inflict it (See Ephesians 2:3-7).

The Humiliation of Satan
Satan is now humiliated and crushed before Almighty God, as he gazes in anger and shock. We are alive and risen to Heaven where we possess our inheritance and now sit at God's right hand - Yeshua the Messiah. We caught a glimpse of his anger and humiliation after he had been rebuked by the Archangel Michael. He believed he had the legal right to have claim over the body of Moses and its location. In Jude 1:9, we read "when the archangel Michael, contending with the devil, judicially argued (disputed) about the body of Moses, he dared not (presume to) bring about an abusive condemnation against him, but (simply) said the Lord rebuke you!" (Amp.Bible).

This is the wonder of God's magnificent power which overrides the authority of Satan. God has chosen us as a tithe of His first fruits and has set us above all His creations. Satan tried to destroy this plan; through humiliation and pride he attempted to 'be like the Most High.' He tried to challenge God's plan which would allow us to be Sons of our Father. This eternal plan was sufficient to cover sin, suffering and death, the result of Adam's choice through disobedience. God has chosen through His Son Yeshua, whose name stands above every other named dignitary; we have now become His bride. We are despised by Satan who despises this plan, however despite his fury, our Father loves us.

JESUS OUR HOPE

Yeshua is our Glorious Hope. An earlier detail in this book, addresses Jesus as God's mighty, uncreated, and eternal life, who dwells in us. When we "sleep" our bodies which have been left behind will rise again, whether we sleep on land or sea. Then those of us who are alive, our bodies will be instantly transformed into new bodies (1 Thess 4:13-18).

This plan of God had been hidden from the angelic rulers and authorities in the heavenly sphere (1 Peter 1:10-12); that the Bride of Yeshua would be of all nationalities. After we have taken our position beside our Elder Brother Yeshua, it will be an awesome event for all rulers, and dignitaries both in the kingdom of light, and of darkness. Once again the everlasting gates will be opened and the King of Glory (Messiah King) will be seen, not alone, we will be sitting beside Him as His Bride. As a result of this triumphant display, and the completion of God's master plan in this area, there will be a major celebration in heaven filled with worship to the One who sits on the throne and to His Son, The Lamb. Once more, we the sons of God will shout for joy.

SONS

Praise God! We belong to Him. We have been chosen before time to inherit the highest title and position as 'Sons of God.' It is above every other name and title - Seraphim, Cherubim, and Archangels, and every other created being. Sons of God will take the highest position above them because we are the family of God (Hebrews 2:12).

And so we are! Beloved, we are (even here and) now God's children, it is not disclosed (made clear) what we shall be (hereafter), but we know that when He comes and is manifested, we shall (as God's children) resemble and be like Him, for we shall see Him just as He (really) is (1 John 3:1-2 Amp. Bible).

The Apostle Paul exclaims in great wonder: "Oh the depth of the riches of the wisdom and knowledge of God, how unsearchable are His judgements and His ways past finding out! For who has known the mind of the Lord? Or who has been His counsellor? Or who has first given to Him and it shall be recompensed unto him again? For of Him and through Him, and to Him, are all things: to whom be glory forever and ever. Amen" (Romans 11: 33-36 KJV).

The Apostle Paul further declares, "For I consider that the sufferings of this present time (this present life) are not worth being compared with the glory which shall be revealed in us. For the anxious longing of the creation waits eagerly for the revealing of the sons of God, for the creation was subjected to futility, not willingly, but because of Him who subjected it, in hope that the creation itself also will be set free from its slavery to corruption into the freedom of the glory of the children of God. For we know that the whole creation groans and suffers the pains of childbirth together until now. And not only this, but also we ourselves, waiting eagerly for our adoption as sons, the redemption of our body. For in hope we have been saved, but hope that is seen is not hope; for who hopes for what he already see? But if we hope for what we do not see, with perseverance we wait eagerly for it" (Romans 8: 18-25 Amp.Bible).

Paul raises two points to our attention:

1. Though the work of Christ and The Holy Spirit have been completed, yet we continually cry for the transformation of our bodies to the glorious immortal one, (Romans 8:20-21) when we shall be "caught away" (1 Thessalonians 4: 16-18).
2. The creation is eagerly waiting for the sons of God to be revealed (Romans 8:14-25; 1 John 3:1-2).

When will the Sons of God be Revealed?

The times and seasons coupled with current world affairs will help us to understand the above question. It is most important to focus on Israel and the Middle East. The Eternal God made an everlasting Covenant with Abraham, and promised that He would destroy the enemies of Israel.

"Now the Lord said to Abram, Go forth from your country and from your relatives and from your father's house to the land which I will show you; and I will make you a great nation, and I will bless you, and make your name great: and so you shall be a blessing: and I will bless those who bless you and the one who curse you I will curse, and in you all the families of the earth will be blessed" (Genesis 12:1-3 The Ryrie Study Bible).

The Prophet Joel foretold "For behold, in those days and at that time when I shall reverse the captivity and restore the fortunes of Judah and Jerusalem, I will gather all nations and will bring them down to the valley of Jehoshaphat, and there I will deal with and execute judgement upon them for (their treatment) of my people and of my heritage Israel, whom they have scattered among the nations and (because) they have divided My land" (Joel 3: 1-2. The Ryrie Study Bible).

The Prophet Zechariah wrote: "Behold a day is coming for the Lord when the spoil taken from you will be divided among you. For I will gather all nations against Jerusalem to battle, and the city will be captured, the houses plundered, the women ravished and half of the city exiled, but the rest of the people will not be cut off from the city. Then the Lord will go forth and fight against those nations, as when He fights on a day of battle. In that day His feet will stand on the Mount of Olives which is in front of Jerusalem on the east; and the Mount of Olives will be split in its middle from east to west by a very large valley, so that half of the mountain will move toward the north and the other half toward the south. You will flee by the valley just as you had before the earthquake in the days of Uzziah king of Judah. Then the Lord, my God, will come, and all the holy ones with Him" (Zechariah 14 NASB).

As we read these two verses, we see something very fascinating. The Holy Spirit revealing part of God's master plan: Yeshua will return not as the Lord of Hosts to defend His people, but with the 'holy ones' the saints and angels. We who have waited for our bodies to be miraculously resurrected, will be present with Him. The disciples who were with Jesus on the Mount of Olives, at His departure into Heaven; they were not aware that they would be returning with Him. The Apostle Jude declares: "Enoch in the seventh generation from Adam prophesied when he said, Behold the Lord comes with his myriads of holy ones (ten thousand of His saints), to execute judgement ......" Jude 14. We will live on this earth once again, and witness God's righteous judgement meted out on the nations who have rejected Him. "And the Lord will be King over all the earth; in that day the Lord will be the only one, and His name the only one" (Zechariah 14:9 Ryrie Study Bible). Then the Lord, who made a covenant with Abraham and also His descendants, Isaac and Jacob, will set up His kingdom here on earth in Jerusalem for a thousand years. It is then that the prophetic words of the Apostle Paul will be fulfilled;

"For I consider that the sufferings of this present time are not worthy to be compared with the glory that is to be revealed in us. For the anxious longing of the creation waits eagerly for the revealing of the sons of God" (Romans 8: 18-19 Ryrie Study Bible).

"See how great a love the Father has bestowed on us, that we would be called children of God: and such we are. For this reason the world does not know us, because it did not know Him" (1 John 3:1 Ryrie Study Bible).

Creation

Paul declares "For the creation was subjected to futility, not of its own will, but because of Him who subjected it, in hope that the creation itself also will be set free from its slavery to corruption into the freedom of the glory of the child of God" (Romans 8:20-21 Ryrie Study Bible). It is evident that the curse on the whole of creation was because of Adam's disobedience; by transgressing the law of God he made a fatal choice which affected the whole world.

When God passed sentence He said "Because you have listened to the voice of your wife and have eaten from the tree about which I commanded you saying, you shall not eat from it; cursed is the ground because of you, in toil you will eat of it all the days your life. Both thorns and thistles it shall grow for you; and you will eat of the plants of the field; by the sweat of your face you will eat bread, till you return to the ground, because of it you were taken; for you are dust and to dust you shall return" (Genesis 3:17-19 Ryrie Study Bible). However, though God had pronounced a curse on creation, yet provision was made in His great master plan; the hope of restoration to its former glory at the appointed time.

The Unveiling of the Sons of God

Yes! The sons of God will be with their Father, the Messiah, to rule with Him in His kingdom here on earth in Jerusalem. "Then I saw thrones, and they sat on them, and judgement was given to them. And I saw the souls of those who had been beheaded because of their testimony of Jesus and because of the word of God, and those who had not worshipped the beast or his image, and had not received the mark on their forehead and on their hand; and they came to life and reigned with Christ for a thousand years" (Rev.20:4 Ryrie Study Bible).

Blessed (happy, to be envied) and holy (spiritually whole, of unimpaired innocence and proved virtue) is the person who takes part (shares) in the first resurrection! Over them the second death exerts no power or authority, but they shall be ministers of God and of Messiah, and they shall rule along with Him a thousand years (Rev. 19: 11-21, 20: 1-7 Amp. Bible).

The Apostle John declares "….Then I saw a new sky (heaven) and a new earth, for the former sky and the former earth had passed away (vanished), and there no longer existed any sea. And I saw the holy city, the New Jerusalem, descending out of heaven from God, all arrayed like a bride beautiful and adorned for her husband.

Then I heard a mighty voice from the throne and I perceived its distinct words, saying, See! The abode of God is with Men, and He will live (encamp, tent) among them, and they shall be His people, and God shall personally be with them and be their God" (Revelation 21:1-3 Amp. Bible).

The land will be restored on that great day of the Lord when He sets up His millennium Kingdom here on earth. His saints now sons of God, will rule and reign with Yeshua the Messiah. This will be the first level of restoration to the earth, however, its full splendour will only be revealed when all things have been fulfilled. There will be a new heaven and a new earth, for the old ones will have passed away and replaced with what I call, the Golden Age of the Kingdom of God and His Son.

Yes! The Ancient of days whose desire that sons and daughters to be born unto Him from mankind, that He could dwell in us through the Spirit of His Son. He has made us worthy to be heirs and joint heirs with

His first begotten Son before all principalities, powers and rulers now and forever, to fulfil the desire of His heart.

Before the beginning of the world, God birthed the **principle of the Essence of Covenant and Grace,** and fulfilled His plan through His Son Yeshua, born of a virgin Mary by means of a **Covenant of Exchange** through which His family of sons and daughters were born unto the Father bearing the nature and character of His Son Yeshua; He exchanged His life for our sins, and took all our failures and limitations. Now we are forgiven through His blood and covered by His righteousness.

"I will make a covenant of peace with them; it shall be an everlasting covenant with them, and I will give blessings to them and multiply them and will set my sanctuary in the midst of them forevermore. My tabernacle or dwelling place also shall be with them and I will be their God, and they shall be my people." (Ezekiel 37:26-27 Amp. Bible).

Thanks be to Yeshua Messiah's sacrifice of Himself that this could be accomplished through The Essence of Covenant and Grace; God's mighty indwelling presence through His Holy Spirit, now residing in His sons and daughters. Amen!

www.ingramcontent.com/pod-product-compliance
Lightning Source LLC
Chambersburg PA
CBHW070117080526
44586CB00013B/1320